Auburn's Unclaimed National Championships

To daddy
from mommy & Marion
we love you!
2014 ♡

Michael Skotnicki

DEDICATION

This book is dedicated to the Auburn Family, and all the teams who have worn the Auburn football uniform since 1892. But it is especially dedicated to the coaches and players of Auburn's 1910, 1913, 1914, 1958, 1983, 1993, and 2004 football teams, who deserve formal recognition as national champions. War Eagle!

CONTENTS

ACKNOWLEDGMENTS

This book is based on historical fact regarding the Auburn University football program, other publicly-available information, and the author's opinions. Most of the information should not be new to knowledgeable Auburn fans. It was gathered from many sources in an attempt to tell as completely as possible the stories of seven specific Auburn football seasons, as well as other Auburn football history, so that the seven seasons are placed in context of over 100 years of Auburn football history.

I am indebted to and grateful to David Housel for the gift of his time spent reading a draft manuscript of this book and offering his comments and sharing information that was needed to help tell the story of Auburn football. It was a great honor to discuss this book with him.

Although certain information in this book was located in newspaper archives and other sources, I am indebted and grateful to the authors of the following books and articles from which much of the historical information was taken. Without their hard work documenting the factual information in those books, this one would not be possible.

"A Tiger Walk Through History: The Complete Story of Auburn Football from 1892 to the Tuberville Era," by Paul Hemphill (2008).

"About them Dawgs! Georgia Football's Most Memorable Teams and Players," by Patrick Garbin (2008).

"AttitUde! A record of the 1993 Auburn Tigers," by Kent Partridge (1993).

"Auburn Football: The Complete History, 1892 – 1987," by Dan W. Hollis (1988). ▼

"Auburn Football," by Elizabeth D. Schafer (2004).

"Auburn University Football Vault: The Story of the Auburn Tigers, 1892 – 2007," by David Housel (2007).

"Champions on the Field," by Lindy's Sports (2004).

"'Fighting Whiskey and Immorality' at Auburn: The Politics of Southern Football, 1919-1927," By Andrew Doyle, in Southern Cultures, Fall 2004, vol. 10, no. 3.

"Greatest Moments in Auburn Tigers Football History," Montgomery Advertiser (2002).

"In the Arena," by Pat Dye (with John Logue) (1992).

"Kick 'Em Big Blue: Memorable Games & Memorable Names in Auburn University Football History," by Al Browning (2001).

"Stop the Presses (so I can get Off): Tales from 40 Years of Sports Writing," by Clyde Bolton.

"The Auburn Tigers of 1957: National Champions," by Paul Reeder (1990).

"The SEC team of the Eighties," by Landon Thomas (2004).

The War Eagle Reader, www.wareaglereader.com, various articles by Jeremy Henderson.

"War Eagle: The Story of Auburn Football," by Clyde Bolton (1987).

"Where Tradition Began: The Centennial History of Auburn Football," by Wayne Hester (1991).

PREFACE: WHAT IS A NATIONAL CHAMPIONSHIP?

Before discussing the seven *unclaimed* national championship seasons of the Auburn University football team that are the primary focus of this book, it's worthwhile to first give some definition to the term "national championship" so that readers understand how that term is used herein. While we know that every fan of a school that plays football wants to win one, what is a national championship?

The first point that must be made is that the National Collegiate Athletic Association does *not* and has *never* itself named any Division I college football team a national champion. While the NCAA may *recognize* certain teams as a national champion, the title has always been awarded by other independent entities, often called "selectors." It should also be recognized that these selectors sometimes disagree and a true consensus as to what team should be recognized as national champion has often been lacking, which has created controversy. For example, while Louisiana State University was the Bowl Championship Series ("BCS") champion in 2003, the University of Southern California also claims to be a 2003 national champion based upon being ranked first in the final poll of the Associated Press, a recognized selector.

An early version of the game of football was first played by colleges in 1869, but it was not widely played outside the East until the 1880's and only became highly popular nationally in the early 1900's. The issue of who was the champion college team for any season was not a national topic of discussion for many decades. When only a small number of schools were fielding football teams, the winner of games between Harvard and Yale was generally considered by those in the East to be the intercollegiate football champion. Then, in the 1880's several sporting magazines began ranking the Eastern teams at the end of the season. Later, regional champions were named by newspapers, and after 1900 certain southern newspapers would name a team the "Champion of the South."

In 1929, former Auburn coach John Heisman argued that the country be divided into four sections, that a champion of each section be chosen, and then that the four teams should play each other to determine a true national champion. He would have the champion of the East play the champion of the South and the champion of the Midwest would play the champion of the West. The winning teams would then play for the national championship. This plan, of course, was never put into action, though it is similar to the four team championship playoff recently adopted by the BCS for the 2014 season and shows Heisman's great foresight about college football.

A few years earlier, in 1926, Frank Dickinson, a professor of economics at the University of Illinois, developed the first mathematical formula for rating college football teams. After determining a national champion for 1926 using this process, he was requested by Notre Dame's coach Knute Rockne to do the same for 1924 and 1925, which resulted in Notre Dame's 10 - 0 team being named by Dickinson the national champion for 1924. This made Notre Dame the first team to claim a "retroactive" national championship for a past season. Professor Dickinson continued his annual rankings through the 1940 season. Soon after Dickinson published his first rankings in 1926, other persons developed similar competing mathematical formula ratings systems and they were widely accepted by college football fans.

However, an alternative to these mathematic rating systems appeared in 1936 when the Associated Press developed a poll based on the votes of sportswriters and broadcasters, who considered themselves to be experts in determining which college football teams were the best. The United Press International developed a competing poll in 1950 that was based on the votes of college coaches, believing that coaches knew how to rate teams better than sportswriters. Though great weight is given today to the A.P. Poll and what is now known as the Coaches Poll, it has never been established that these human polls are more accurate in choosing a national champion than the various selectors who used mathematical formulas, especially those selectors approved by the NCAA. In fact, the human polls cannot eliminate the factor of rankings being in part a popularity contest. Despite this, the human polls became more accepted over time as they were actively pushed onto the public by the sports media from where they originated.

An inherent flaw in the system used by the A.P. and the U.P.I. is that the human ranking of teams were sometimes based entirely on a team winning that week's game and by what margin of victory, rather than including a measure of the strength of the opponent, which is an integral part of the older mathematical formulas. The factor of strength of schedule was also included in the more sophisticated mathematical formulas that could be developed once computers were invented, such as the newer ratings systems developed by Richard Billingsley in 1970, and even more recently by Jeff Sagarin and others, including the New York Times.

Six computer polls, along with the results of certain human polls, have been included in the formula for determining the teams to play in the Bowl Championship Series ("BCS") championship game. However, even some of those computer formulas have flaws as they include preseason ratings of teams in the scoring system, such that *perceptions* of the strength of teams – before any game is played – has influence on the final outcome of the ratings, which has the potential of creating a self-fulfilling prophecy. This is best represented by the 2004 BCS championship game between the University of Southern California and the University of Oklahoma. Those teams began the season ranked first and second in the human polls, which resulted in them maintaining the same spots in the final, pre-championship game BCS standings even though Auburn actually played a more difficult schedule, simply because Auburn began the season ranked seventeenth.

While the "national championship game" format of the BCS was a positive step toward determining a sole national champion as compared to the results of pairing disparate teams in various bowl games, the four-team playoff system set to begin with the 2014 season – which should be called the Heisman system – will be a further improvement that should help to determine a true college football champion. Until then, as most college football experts recognize, a college football national championship is and has always been "mythical" because there is no way of truly determining which team is best and every selector is simply offering an opinion.

In fact, the term "mythical" was to describe the college football championship as far back as 1921. Accordingly, more than one college team may be able to make a legitimate claim to the title of national champion for any given year and, until the best teams are placed in a playoff system so that they can compete directly against each other for a national championship, as is done in basketball and baseball, college football fans will have to accept the likelihood of more than one team being ablet to legitimately claim a national championship for any given year.

The relevant question for discussion and debate among fans that cannot truly be answered then becomes whether a university's claim to a national championship in any given year is more legitimate than another's, based on the facts of that season. For example, who is the true national champion of the 2003 season, A.P. poll champion Southern California (12-1) or BCS championship game winner Louisiana State (13-1)? The matter is mostly one of opinion.

Moreover, the further back in time one goes, the more difficult it becomes to decide the question because there were few intersectional games and it is difficult to compare strengths of teams from different regions without common opponents. Thus, the debate may never be settled, and perhaps that has been good for college football.

1

INTRODUCTION

Auburn University has fielded intercollegiate football teams since 1892, and its Athletic Department presently claims the national championships won for the 1957 and 2010 college football seasons. In addition to those two national championships, Auburn is widely recognized as being one of the colleges where John Heisman, for whom the Heisman Trophy is named, was head football coach and as being the only one of those colleges to later produce a winner of that award. In fact, Auburn has now had three winners of this award given annually to the most outstanding player in college football. Just outside Jordan-Hare Stadium on the Auburn campus, larger-than-life statues of Pat Sullivan (1971), Vincent "Bo" Jackson (1985), and Cameron Newton (2010) now tower over visitors.

However, the sports media covering the Auburn football team, both within Alabama and nationally, have not bothered to learn more about the grand history of Auburn football than those two national championship teams and the three Heisman Trophy winners. As a whole, the sports media does not give enough credit to Auburn for its great tradition as a college football power over the last 120 years, which I would argue is only second to the University of Alabama in the SEC. Even Auburn's own Athletic Department, while acknowledging the winning tradition and history of many All-American and award-winning players, fails to promote all the championships that Auburn's football teams have won, or that Auburn ranks twelfth in all-time wins among Division I colleges. Even though former head coach Gene Chizik reminded his players that "Auburn was great long before you got here," the Athletic Department hasn't done enough to recognize all the championships won by earlier Auburn teams.

Although other universities claim national championships based on selectors other than the Associated Press, United Press International/Coaches Poll, and the BCS Championships - especially ones recognized by the NCAA as acceptable selectors, such as Richard Billingsley's computer rankings - Auburn has taken a very conservative approach and has limited itself to claiming only the 1957 A.P. and 2010 titles. For example, under Auburn's self-imposed standard, Michigan could only claim to have won two national championships, but claims eleven. Notre Dame could only claim to have won eight, but claims eleven; Pittsburgh could only claim to have won two, but claims nine; Ohio State could only claim five, but claims seven; Michigan State could only claim to have won two, but claims six; Tennessee could only claim two, but claims six, Georgia Tech could only claim one, but claims four, and Mississippi could not claim any, but claims three.

According to an article by *Birmingham News* sportswriter Jon Solomon that was published on January 6, 2010, the reason the University of Alabama claims fifteen national championships is because Wayne Atcheson, who was the Sports Information Director from 1983 to 1987, decided to claim five additional national championships, based upon retroactive championship selectors, in addition to those national championships won during the "Bear" Bryant era. Thus, sometime in 1986 the number of national championships claimed by Alabama jumped overnight from six to eleven. Alabama has since added national championships in 1992, 2009, 2011, and 2012. In the *Birmingham News* article, Atcheson noted that his intent in adding five national championships to Alabama's total was to "make Alabama football the best it could be and make it as great as it could possibly be."

This book is a response to the self-imposed standard for claiming national championships that Auburn's Athletic Department has adopted and provides information about Auburn's *unclaimed* National Championship seasons in 1910, 1913, 1914, 1958, 1983, 1993, and 2004. Auburn has been recognized as a national champion for these years by various national championship selectors, and the 1913, 1983, and 1993 teams are officially recognized as national champions for those seasons by the NCAA. Why shouldn't the Auburn Athletic Department also seek to make Auburn as great as it possibly could be? Why shouldn't Auburn claim seven more national championships, or at least the three additional ones recognized by the NCAA?

This book is not about the 1957 and 2010 national championships; it is about Auburn's seven *unclaimed* national championships. While the claim to a national championship in each of those seasons is not undisputed, until the playoff system recently approved by the NCAA is implemented, the idea of a national champion is mythical, and there is no compelling reason why Auburn should not claim these national championships.

A strong argument can be made for recognizing each Auburn team noted as a national champion for those seven years and in each instance at least one recognized selector has deemed Auburn's team worthy of being called a national champion. All of these Auburn Tiger teams were dominant against their peers, were chosen as a national champion by a recognized selector, and were either (a) undefeated, (b) conference champions, or (c) both. This is an appropriate standard for claiming a national championship.

By comparison, this standard cannot be met for every one of the fifteen national championships claimed by the University of Alabama. Alabama's Athletic Department officially claims to have won a national championship in 1941, a season in which it finished 9 - 2, was shut out by both Mississippi State University and Vanderbilt University, finished third in the Southeastern Conference standings, and was ranked 20th in the final Associated Press poll.

Despite those undeniable facts that suggest a good but not great season, Alabama claims a national championship for 1941 because under the ranking system of a single selector, Deke Houlgate of Los Angeles, it was the highest rated team. Alabama's claim of the 1941 National Championship, resting solely on the opinion of a single recognized selector to inflate a third-place conference finish into a national championship, sets a fairly low bar for a claim of a national championship season. That's not to say Alabama's claim is illegitimate; it's just as legitimate as any claim made by a university to a national championship based on Houlgate, who began his college football ranking system in the 1930's and named champions for every season between 1885 and 1949.

Using the more difficult standard described further above, there is a strong argument for Auburn claiming a national championship in each of the seven seasons discussed in this book. These seven additional national championship seasons should not only be embraced by Auburn's alumni and fans, they should be formally recognized by the Athletic Department such that Auburn would then claim nine national championships.

While the Auburn Media Guide does note in the section relating to historical schedule results that the 1913, 1983, 1993, and 2004 teams were named national champions by one or more selectors, the Athletic Department should do more than simply make that notation. It should raise national championship banners in Jordan-Hare Stadium for all the teams noted in this book, just as for the 1957 and 2010 teams. The great coaches and players of these seven other teams, who trained so long and fought so hard on the gridiron, both within this last decade and more than 100 years ago, deserve that respect and acknowledgement of their tremendous accomplishments on the gridiron.

Auburn University would not be alone if it took the step of formally recognizing these seven teams from its past as national champions. As previously noted, Alabama added five past national championships during the 1980's. More recently, in 2004, the University of Southern California formally claimed its 1939 Pacific Coast Conference co-champion team, which had an 8 – 0 - 2 record, as a national champion based on the Dickinson ratings.

Just last year, Texas A & M University and the University of Minnesota claimed additional national championships based the rankings of recognized retroactive selectors. Texas A & & M claimed a national championship for 1919, a season where it finished 10 - 0 and won a Southwest Conference championship, and was named national champion by retroactive selector the National Championship Foundation. Texas A & M also claimed a national championship for 1927, a season where it finished 8 – 0 - 1, won the Southwest Conference championship, and was named a retroactive national champion by Jeff Sagarin's ratings. Minnesota claimed a national championship for the 1904 season in which it finished 13 – 0 (though it only played five major teams), was Big Ten co-champion, and is recognized as national champion for that year by the retroactive selector the Billingsley Report.

Auburn should join these other universities and give the seven teams discussed in this book the respect and honor they deserved by officially claiming a national championship for those seasons. Certainly, Auburn University should not impose upon itself a stricter standard for recognizing a national championship than that used by the NCAA, and it should at a minimum join the NCAA in formally recognizing and claiming Coach Donahue's 1913 team, Coach Dye's 1983 team, and Coach Bowden's 1993 squad team as national champions.

The opinions expressed in this book are those of the author alone, and not Auburn University. This book has not been endorsed by nor is authorized by the Auburn University Athletic Department. Readers of this book can form their own opinions as to whether Auburn University should claim these seven additional national championships, and this book is simply intended to present information about the 1910, 1913, 1914, 1958, 1983, 1993, and 2004 Auburn football seasons to the public and to serve as a resource for discussion and debate.

2

COACH JOHN HEISMAN, COACH "IRON MIKE" DONAHUE, AND THE 1910 NATIONAL CHAMPIONSHIP SEASON

Auburn's winning tradition dates back to the very birth of college football in the Deep South. In 1892, Auburn played and won the seminal collegiate football game in the Deep South, played against the University of Georgia in Atlanta's Piedmont Park. Other early Auburn football teams are widely known for being led by legendary coach John Heisman from 1895 to 1899.

Heisman coached Auburn to a successful 12 – 4 - 1 record using guile and trickery, such a double and even triple laterals during a play, to win games while fielding a squads that were outmatched in size and talent. While at Auburn he originated both the use of a long snap count to draw the defense offsides and the "hidden ball" trick play, variations of which are still used today. Heisman also strongly advocated legalization of the forward pass as a means to spread the players across the field and lessen the brutality of the game. The death of a Georgia player in 1897, along with deaths of other players, almost led to the banning of the sport of football. Passing plays helped take brutality out of the game and when the forward pass was eventually legalized in 1906, it was often called a "Heisman pass."

Heisman, who was somewhat of a coaching vagabond, left Auburn for Clemson University in 1900, moved on to Georgia Tech in 1904, and eventually was head coach at eight colleges. At Georgia Tech, where Heisman coached until 1919, his teams would rival Auburn for dominance in Deep South football, yet he would only gain five wins against Auburn in fifteen tries.

The Auburn coach that got the best of Heisman while at Georgia Tech was "Iron Mike" Donahue, who was also later named a member of the College Football Hall of Fame. Donahue, who was from an Irish immigrant family, had played quarterback at Yale University, a dominant Eastern team of that era. Yale had a record of 45-2-2 in Donahue's four years at Yale. Donahue, at the young age of twenty-five, accepted the offer to bring Eastern-style football to Auburn.

With no head coaching experience and little in the way of what could be called a football program, Donahue was expected to struggle. However, a surprising 7 - 0 record in his first season against a relatively soft schedule created great excitement and interest in the football team. But two losing seasons against tougher competition followed and from 1904 to 1906 Auburn's cumulative record was a disappointing 12 – 9 - 1. Auburn people wondered if Donahue's first season had simply been a fluke instead of a preview of what lay ahead.

Donahue recognized the problem of building a consistently winning football program at a small rural college so distant from the southern cities of Birmingham, Nashville, and Atlanta, where high schools had begun to field football teams. The star players from the high schools headed to the local colleges, Alabama, Vanderbilt, and Georgia Tech, but Auburn had no such feeder system for football talent. Nor could Auburn afford to offer scholarships to football players, as Sewanee had begun doing in the 1890s to attract players from across the South and build a program that was dominant for a time. Donahue realized that if he was to be successful at Auburn, he was going to have to find another way to field a winning team.

In an unusual move, Donahue stepped down as the head coach for the 1907 season to concentrate on being the Athletic Director and building a foundation for the football program. His answer to the lack of experienced high school players was to create an intramural program that would teach football to the raw, athletic country boys that enrolled at Auburn. Under this system, each class, from freshman to senior, fielded a team coached by varsity players and competed against each other. The best players of the intramural teams were then elevated to the varsity team.

Donahue was very hard on his players in practice and demanded great effort and execution. He was known for saying that having the "will to prepare" was far more important than the "will to win" because without preparation there can be no lasting success. Sportswriter Zipp Newman of the *Birmingham News* wrote that Donahue "made Auburn a power in Southern football along with Vanderbilt, Sewanee, and Georgia Tech" using "greener material" than the other coaches, and that "[h]e took raw-boned boys, many of who had never played or even seen high school football, and molded them into hard-charging, fierce blocking and running teams."

One of Donahue's assistants, W.S. Keinholz coached the improving 1907 team to a fine 6 – 2 - 1 record. However,

Donahue, who had served as an assistant to Keinholz that year, returned as head coach for the 1908 season and for fourteen more years. During the Donahue era, Auburn became a dominant team in Southern football, winning several Southern Intercollegiate Athletic Association "SIAA" Championships.

Donahue was known for his integrity, as he refused to use "ringers," the traveling professional players who were being hired by colleges across the South. The use of ringers in the South was so common that 1907 became known as the "season of the ringers" and the practice did not completely cease until years later when a rule was adopted by the Southern Conference that a football player had to be a student for a full year before he was eligible to play. Instead of hiring ringers, Donahue relied upon his intramural system, kept the Auburn program above reproach, and built a program that eventually succeeded Vanderbilt as the preeminent Southern football power.

The respect given to Donahue's efforts at the time to keep the game "clean" is reflected by the fact that although Auburn finished 6 - 1 in 1908, newspapers named Auburn the "Champion of the South" despite the fact both LSU and Vanderbilt had gone undefeated. Auburn's sole loss was to LSU, a team that sportswriter Grantland Rice of the Nashville Tennessean exposed as having seven ringers on its roster. LSU's ringers included star player George "Doc" Fenton, who was from Pennsylvania and who had been the leading LSU player in its 10 – 2 victory over Auburn that year. In 1909, Donahue led Auburn to a 6 – 2 season, with one loss being by just by a single point to Sewannee. The 1910 season would prove to be Donahue's best team to that point, going 6 – 1, sharing the SIAA championship with

Vanderbilt and later being recognized as a national champion.

Though no trophy is named for Coach Mike Donahue, he was clearly more successful than John Heisman when they went head-to-head for fifteen years at Auburn and Georgia Tech. Donahue defeated Heisman in ten of fifteen games. Donahue was also inducted into the College Football Hall of Fame in its inaugural class in 1951, three years before Heisman.

Coach Donahue was also the equal of Coach Dan McGugin at Vanderbilt, which was an established football power. McGugin took over as Vanderbilt's head coach in 1904 and began using the same "hurry up" style of offense as his mentor, Fielding Yost of Michigan. From 1904 through 1907 and from 1910 through 1912, McGugin's Vanderbilt team was either SIAA champion or co-champion. Yet in games against a McGugin-coached Vanderbilt team, Donahue went 4 – 5 – 1, with one loss occurring by a single point in a 7 - 6 score when Auburn's kicker missed the tying extra point.

College football in this era was well beyond the days of the "flying wedge." Complex offensive formations, such as the single wing and double wing developed by Glenn "Pop" Warner, were the strategy of the day. Like today, formations were disguised to the defense by pre-snap shifts. Plays included players in motion, fake handoffs, single and double laterals, and reverses. Some teams even used a no huddle offense that allowed for a greater number of plays in a game and thus more scoring.

While passes were not plentiful, the pass play had been legalized in 1906 and teams in this era commonly used the pass at least as a trick play and more frequently when the team had an accurate passer. One formation that was used occasionally by passing teams was a precursor to the modern "shotgun" formation that was called the "short punt" formation because the quarterback would line up to receive the snap in a position shorter than he would if he were to punt the ball.

While Coach Heisman is acclaimed as an innovator of the game, Coach Donahue was as well. Donahue believed that the best offense was a great defense and his teams were known for their staunch attacking defense. He used a seven man defensive line that featured "smashing ends," who lined up on the outer edge of the offensive formation to contain that side of the field. He coached his defensive ends to get across the line as quickly as possible and disrupt the play before it could develop. Today, this would be called a 7 – 2 – 2 defense, or a "7 box." His defenses, referred to by sportswriters as being "strong as iron," gave him his nickname, "Iron Mike."

Donahue's favorite offensive formation was known as the "Line Divide," which was a variant of the T-formation he had played in at Yale. In that era, with little passing threat, defenses crowded the line of scrimmage such that there was often very little room for a offensive player to run. The "Line Divide" helped solve that problem. The formation usually featured an unbalanced line, and the gaps between the linemen were sometimes as wide as three yards. In this early form of a spread formation, the backs would line up in an I-formation, then would shift before the snap. The wide splits in the line helped to stretch the defense from sideline to sideline and opened the middle of the field for Donahue's staple play, the fullback dive. It was the play that made a star of Bradley Streit and later Auburn fullbacks. Donahue also believed in running the same play over again until it was stopped, and in many games he played three fullbacks because they tired from carrying the ball so often.

Atlanta Constitution sportswriter Ed Danforth wrote of the Auburn teams during the Donahue era: "You were nobody until you had beaten Auburn. That was the place card at the head of the table." While Donahue Drive, where Auburn's traditional "Tiger Walk" to Jordan-Hare Stadium occurs, is named for Coach Donahue, much more should be done by Auburn's Athletic Department to bring recognition to his tenure as Auburn's head football coach and the National Championships and SIAA Championships his teams earned.

Three of Donahue's teams -- 1910, 1913, and 1914 -- have been named as national champions by various recognized retroactive selectors. The 1910 team was selected as a national champion by retroactive selectors, the Maxwell Ratings of Loren Maxwell and the College Football Rankings of Kyle Matschke, who have both used a mathematical system to select national champions for college football beginning with the 1869 season. The following is a description of Auburn's 1910 national championship season.

Some Southeastern Conference football fans feel the expansion of the conference to 14 teams in 2012 has made it too large. However, in 1910, the SIAA, a precursor to the SEC, was composed of more than twenty colleges. The members of the SIAA in 1910 included: Alabama, Auburn, Birmingham-Southern, Citadel, Centre, Clemson, Georgia, Georgia Tech, Howard (Samford), Furman, Kentucky, LSU, Memphis, Mercer, Mississippi, Mississippi A&M (Mississippi State), Sewanee, Tennessee, Tulane, Vanderbilt, and Virginia. Of course football was a bit different in 1910.

The forward pass was used less often, though Donahue was the first coach in the South to run a pass play (in game against Sewanee) after it was legalized in 1906.

Auburn's 1910 team, like all of Iron Mike's teams, was exceptionally strong on defense. For the entire season, the defense yielded only nine points, all scored by the University of Texas late in the fourth quarter of a game played in Austin. Unfortunately, Auburn was unable to muster a score in that game and it was the team's only loss that season.

Auburn's 1910 season opened with one of its very few games at home. Auburn beat Mississippi State by the score of 6 - 0 in a defensive slugfest. Mississippi State fielded a strong team in 1910, going 7 - 2, and the victory for Auburn was a good omen for a strong season. Freshman quarterback Kirk Newell had two big plays for Auburn, first by completing a long pass and then by a long run on a sweep play that set up the winning five-yard touchdown run by fullback Bradley Streit.

Streit, one of Auburn's All-Southern team selections in 1910, would lead Auburn and all the teams in the South in the number of touchdowns scored that season. He later transferred to Princeton University and starred for Princeton in the 1913 season. At Princeton, Streit proved just as dominate against the supposedly superior Eastern schools, was voted the best player on the Princeton squad that year. Streit, who later became a successful businessman in Canada and endowed a scholarship at Princeton, stated that his 1910 Auburn team was much superior to his 1913 Princeton team. Streit's ability to run through the defenses of the powerful Eastern teams in 1913, after being only one of the stars on Auburn's 1910 squad, evidences the great strength of play from Auburn in 1910 and lends credence to its recognition as a national champion.

Auburn's next game was on October 15 in Birmingham against Howard College (Samford University), a fellow SIAA member. Auburn completely outclassed Howard, and won 77 - 0. As one author of a book on Auburn football described it, "Kirk Newell ran the opening kickoff all the way for a touchdown and the deluge was on." Newell scored twice, while Streit and halfback John Davis, the Tigers' other All-Southern back, each scored four touchdowns.

On October 22, Auburn returned home to play Clemson, in the second and what would be the final home game that season. After having run roughshod over overmatched Howard, it was apparent that Auburn, at least on offense, was not mentally prepared for a more difficult opponent, as they played sloppily and lost several fumbles. Yet the Auburn defense was commanding and the game was never in doubt. Auburn scored three touchdowns and won 17 - 0. Auburn's first touchdown was set up by a long Kirk Newell punt return. Bradley Streit powered in from inside the five-yard line and Auburn had all the points it needed. Later in the game John Davis scored on a short run and W.G. Sherling recovered a punt for a touchdown that had been blocked by lineman "Sheep" Lamb. Auburn was clearly the top Tiger that day.

With a 3-0 record in SIAA games, Auburn boarded the train for the long ride to Austin, Texas for an October 29 game against a strong Longhorn team that finished its season with a 6 - 2 record. This was one of the first intersectional games in Southern college football and Texas was considered the top team in the Southwest. In that era, travel was by train, an extremely slow and grueling means of crossing the country. Passenger trains traveled at less than twenty-five miles per hour and with the need to change trains, a trip from Auburn to Austin took several days. Little opportunity existed for practice as professors traveled with the team and kept the players busy with their studies.

Despite the rigor of Auburn's long train travel, the Auburn versus Texas game was an epic, scoreless battle between two evenly matched teams through the first three quarters. Auburn played aggressively, led by Bill Streit's "phenomenal" long runs through the middle of Texas' defense, but an incomplete fourth down pass and a missed field goal kept Auburn scoreless in the first half. Auburn's last scoring opportunity was with five minutes left, when the Tigers failed to score on a fourth down at the Texas five yard line. While Texas was able to freely substitute fresh players, Auburn's men could no longer overcome the fatigue of a nearly 700 mile train ride simply by their will to win. With only a squad of sixteen players that had traveled for the game, there was little opportunity for Auburn to substitute in an era when players played both offense and defense. Texas finally broke the scoreless tie with a long field goal in the final minutes and then used a surprise onside kickoff. A Texas player recovered the kick and ran sixty yards for a touchdown to put the game away with a 9 - 0 victory. The Galveston Daily News described the game as "the hardest fought and best played game in the South this season."

Weary from the train trip to Texas and the exhausting game, the Tiger football team nonetheless boarded their train and continued straight to Atlanta for a November 5 game against Georgia Tech, then coached by John Heisman. Even with players who hadn't practiced since the Texas game, Donahue got the best of Heisman in a 16 - 0 victory. After having been the victim of an on-side kick against Texas, this time Donahue used the trick play against Georgia Tech to set up a touchdown run by Ernest Manning in the first quarter. Auburn also got second-half touchdowns from Bradley Streit and John Davis to put the game out of reach and show clear dominance over a strong Georgia Tech team.

With no rest for the weary, the Auburn team played on the road once again the following week. The November 12 game against Tulane University was played in New Orleans before 8,000 spectators. With powerful running from Streit and Davis, Auburn romped to a 33 - 0 victory that would have been much greater had the game not been played on a field of unpacked sand that Tulane had added to its playing field in order to slow Auburn's runners.

After a week off, Auburn traveled again to Savannah for a Thanksgiving Day game against the University of Georgia before 5,000 fans, including the governors of both states. With Alabama no longer on Auburn's schedule after 1907 (Auburn led the series 6 – 4 - 1 at that time), Georgia had become Auburn's chief rival, and the final game of the season would decide important bragging rights as well as the SIAA championship. In a story about the upcoming game, the *Atlanta Constitution* warned fans that Georgia would face an Auburn team that was "the strongest team that has ever appeared on a southern gridiron."

Auburn showed that high praise was true as it outplayed Georgia from the start. A Georgia player fumbled the opening kickoff and Auburn recovered on the ten yard line. John Davis took the football in for a touchdown on the next play. Auburn's defense completely stifled the Georgia offense. The Tigers shut down the running of All-Southern halfback Bob McWhorter, allowed only one pass completion, and blocked two punts. Several players contributed to Auburn's offensive success, which would have been even greater had not the game been played on a "heavy field" that slowed Auburn's runners. In addition to Davis's first quarter touchdown, Bradley Streit powered in for two scores on "line plunges" and Auburn earned a dominating 26 - 0 victory over a strong Bulldog team that finished its season 6 – 2 - 1 while holding five opponents without a score.

For the season, Auburn outscored its opponents 175 to 9 and was the most dominant team in the South. Only SIAA co-champion Vanderbilt (both 5 - 0) could possibly contest that claim. Yet, when the sports editor of the Atlanta Constitution newspaper proposed a championship game in Atlanta between Auburn and Vanderbilt and issued each school a formal invitation, Auburn accepted but Vanderbilt declined. Vanderbilt's hesitancy to play left no doubt in the minds of Southerners that Auburn was the stronger team.

Led by All-Southern runners Bradley Streit and John Davis, All-Southern center E.L Caton, and rising star Kirk Newell, the 1910 team had power and speed on offense as well as an attacking defense characteristic of Donahue squads, and it is deserving of the title of national champion.

One factor in Auburn being named national champion by the Maxwell Ratings despite one loss may be that Auburn won convincingly while playing five of its seven games on the road against strong competition. In that era, many teams modified the playing field to neutralize the advantages of their opponent, such as Tulane adding loose sand or letting the grass grow as high as possible. Auburn played games from Savannah to Austin, Texas, and New

Orleans in between, and overcame that burden all but one time against a strong Texas team.

The other teams recognized as champions for that year, Harvard University (8 - 0 - 1) and the University of Pittsburgh (9 - 0), each comfortably played all but one of their games at home. Moreover, Pittsburgh, whose undefeated record may appear impressive, played only two teams with winning records while Auburn, like Harvard, played five such teams. Thus, as best one can measure, Auburn was the equal of Harvard and Pittsburgh in 1910.

Some sports writers and commentators have opined that the level of football played by Eastern teams such as Harvard, Pittsburgh, Yale, and others was much better than that played by Southern teams. Of course, that is mere speculation since there were very few intersectional games in that era between Eastern and Southern colleges, and when there were such games it was generally the Southern team that traveled by train to play on the Eastern team's home field, thus starting each game at a distinct disadvantage.

While it may have been true that Eastern teams were better in the 1890s, when football was new to the South, by the second decade of the 20th Century that was no longer the case. The supposed Eastern dominance of college football was more likely simply a bias against the South lingering from the Civil War. For example, the Eastern sportswriters picking annual All-American teams refused to name any Southern Player an All-American until just one, Georgia's Bob McWhorter, was chosen in 1913.

The fact is, by 1910, there was little difference between the best teams in the South and those in the East or other parts of the country. By this time the college coaches in the South were no longer amateurs. Donahue had starred at

Yale brought an Eastern-style of football with him when he arrived at Auburn in 1904. By 1910, he had developed a skilled and experienced team that could rival any team in the country. Also in 1904, John Heisman took the job at Georgia Tech and Dan McGugin, an assistant to famous Michigan coach Fielding Yost, started at Vanderbilt. These three men, all trained in football at established Northern football programs, became the elite coaches in the South and by six years later in 1910 had lifted the play of football in the South to be on par with teams elsewhere in the country.

For example, Vanderbilt, with whom Auburn shared the 1910 SIAA championship, played a strong Yale team to a scoreless tie that year. Bradley Streit, just one of the stars on the 1910 team, would go on to be just as dominant a player at Princeton University in 1913, where he was described as the "luminary," "an irresistible line smasher," a "185 pound steamroller," who would lead all of the East in scoring. And when Northern powers Ohio State University and the Carlisle Indian School traveled south later in the decade as prohibitive favorites, Auburn tied Ohio State and beat Carlisle by a touchdown.

In sum, Auburn is a national champion for 1910 because the team was SIAA co-champion; shut out all but one opponent; played most games distant from Auburn; was recognized by an Atlanta newspaper as "the strongest team that has ever appeared on a southern gridiron," and was later chosen as national champion for that year by two retroactive selectors. The 1910 Auburn team, SIAA champion, is deserving of the title of national champion and that championship should be claimed by Auburn's Athletic Department with a banner in Jordan-Hare Stadium.

3

THE 1913 NATIONAL CHAMPIONSHIP SEASON

After an SIAA co-championship in 1910, Auburn stumbled a bit to a 5 – 2 – 1 record in 1911, with non-conference losses at Texas A&M and at the University of Texas. However, Auburn was again dominant against its SIAA opponents, including an 11 – 6 victory over Georgia Tech in which Ted Arnold intercepted a Tech pass and returned it 105 yards for a touchdown. Only a disappointing scoreless tie with Georgia prevented Auburn from sharing another championship with Vanderbilt. Although a healthy team would have been favored against Georgia, Coach Donahue, star Kirk Newell, and several other players were sickened with typhoid fever and a patchwork squad was sent to Savannah. In fact, Coach Donahue, hospitalized, near death, and delirious, insisted upon writing a letter to be read to his team before the game, urging them to fight and win for "old Auburn." Inspired by Donahue's words, which reportedly brought the players to tears, the undermanned team managed to fight Georgia to the scoreless tie.

The 1912 squad started 7 – 0, including a 27 – 7 whipping of Georgia Tech that included an 80 yard touchdown run by Kirk Newell and gave rise to championship hopes once again. However, the Tigers closed with a 7 – 7 tie with Vanderbilt, who had finally agreed to play Auburn in Birmingham instead of Nashville, and then a

12 – 6 upset loss to Georgia and its star Bob McWhorter that ended the team's chance for another SIAA championship.

Donahue had perhaps the best squad of his Auburn coaching career in 1913, and his Tigers certainly lived up to their name by going 8 - 0 while playing every game against an SIAA team, the most difficult schedule in the South. With only two games at home, Auburn outscored its opponents 224 - 6. Auburn placed six players on the eleven player All-Southern team, including left halfback Kirk Newell.

Newell had starred at quarterback on the 1910 SIAA co-champion and national champion team but was moved to halfback in 1913 when Ted Arnold showed he could handle quarterback duties. Newell was nicknamed "The Runt" because of his five-foot, seven-inch, 140-pound size, but like many great runners today, he had great leg strength. Tacklers would bounce off him despite his diminutive stature. In an article about the LSU game in 1912, a Mobile newspaper described how difficult Newell was to tackle: "Time after time a great LSU defender would hit his thick legs, only to bounce off, somersault and get up to see Newell's back flying farther down the field." Donahue later proclaimed Newell "the greatest player I ever coached." Newell finished the 1913 season with 1707 combined yards in just eight games, which was 46 percent of the team's total of 3680 yards in those games. He finished his four year Auburn career with a total of 5,800 yards rushing, 350 yards passing, and 1200 yards returning kicks.

The 1913 Auburn team is named as a national champion by at least six retroactive selectors. These are James Howell's Power Ratings System, the Billingsley Report, the Hatch Mathematical College Football Rankings, 1st-N-Goal, the Dolphin Historical College Football

Rankings, and the College Football Rankings of Kyle Matschke. In the Official NCAA Records book, Auburn is listed as sharing the 1913 national championship with Harvard University and the University of Chicago based upon Billingsley's ratings. Billingsley, an NCAA-sanctioned selector, has called for Auburn to claim a national championship for 1913 (and 1983, as well). That award makes Auburn the first Southern team to have won a national championship.

The SIAA had changed a bit by 1913 and the members then were Alabama, Auburn, Centre, Citadel, Clemson, Florida, Georgia, Georgia Tech, Kentucky, LSU, Mississippi, Mississippi State, Sewanee, Tennessee, Texas A&M, Tulane, Vanderbilt, and Virginia. The following is a description of that 1913 National Championship season.

Auburn opened the season on October 4 with a home game against Mercer that became a runaway 53 - 0 victory. Kirk Newell led the way, scoring three touchdowns, including the final score of the game on a 70-yard punt return. Auburn had a powerful offensive line that was anchored by All-Southern linemen Frank Lockwood and Jim Thigpen, as well as center John Pitts, who was nicknamed "Boozer" in fun because he was a teetotaler and the son of a Baptist preacher. With a strong line, Auburn relied on a dominating running game. In addition to Newell, fullback Frank "Red" Harris, quarterback Ted Arnold, fullback Bill Christopher, and halfback Richard "Bull" Kearley all made touchdowns against an overwhelmed Mercer defense.

After destroying Mercer's team, on October 11, Auburn hosted the University of Florida team for its second and final home game. Florida had beaten Florida Southern by the score of 144 – 0 the week before and were considered a formidable foe. However, once again, Auburn completely dominated, winning 55 - 0. Donahue's attacking defense allowed Florida only one first down. Meanwhile, points came easy to the Auburn offense against Florida, as seven different players scored touchdowns.

On October 18, Auburn traveled for an away game against Clemson and came away with a 20 - 0 shutout. Like the defense, the Auburn running game was again dominant. Bill Christopher, Red Harris, and Kirk Newell all made touchdown runs.

On October 26, Auburn played in Birmingham against a strong Mississippi State team that would not be beaten again and would finish its season 6 – 1 - 1. Kirk Newell was the star of the game. He had a short first quarter touchdown run, followed by a 60 yard touchdown run in the second quarter, and then a 60 yard punt return in the third quarter that set up another score. The final tally was 34 - 0 and Donahue's team was halfway to an undefeated season.

Next up for Auburn was a game in Mobile against LSU on November 1. LSU had another strong team, but when fullback Frank Hart scored from the six yard line in the third quarter, Auburn had all the points it would need, winning by the score of 7 - 0. The game would be LSU's only loss, and it would finish with a 6 - 1 - 2 record.

The schedule would not get any easier for Auburn. A game in Atlanta against Heisman's Georgia Tech team was up next on November 8. Tech and Auburn battled through a scoreless first half, but then Auburn took control with a 25 yard touchdown run by Kirk Newell that completed a long drive. Frank Hart finished the scoring with a great 85 yard touchdown run and then a 10 yard touchdown in the fourth quarter. The final score was a 20 - 0 victory over a Georgia Tech team that would finish its season with a 7 – 2 record.

Auburn's defense had yet to yield a single point in six games and Newell was playing as well as any halfback in the South, but people still had doubts about the strength of this Auburn team, as it had been undefeated at the same point of the season in 1912 and stumbled to finish with a tie and loss against Vanderbilt and Georgia. The most important games of 1913 lay ahead.

On November 15, Auburn traveled to Birmingham to play Vanderbilt team, defending SIAA champions, before 10,000 fans crowded into Rickwood Field. Able to tap into the local Nashville high school teams for talented players, McGugin had quickly established Vanderbilt as a Southern football power when he arrived in 1904 and he, Donahue, and Heisman were the premier coaches in the South during the first two decades of the Twentieth Century. Newspaper articles about the upcoming game billed it as "the South's Greatest Game" and Vanderbilt was a slight favorite.

After the squads had battled to a tie the year before, Coach Donahue would accept nothing less than a victory in 1913. In the first quarter, Auburn forced a fumble and took possession of the ball at midfield. A pair of runs by Newell and Hart brought the ball to the Vanderbilt twenty-four yard line. A Vanderbilt holding penalty took the ball down to the nine yard line and Auburn took a 7 - 0 lead when on third down Hart powered in from the seven yard line and Ted Arnold made the extra point. McGugin dug into his bag of tricks just before the half and Vanderbilt scored on a 40 yard halfback pass that was run off the Statue of Liberty play, a trick play where the quarterback fakes a pass while actually slipping the ball to a runner. But Vanderbilt's kicker missed the extra point and Auburn held a slim 7 - 6 lead at halftime.

In the second half, Newell returned a Vanderbilt punt for 40 yards, but Auburn could not capitalize on the great field position and the game wore on as a defensive struggle with the teams repeatedly trading punts. Wanting to wear down the Vanderbilt defense in the fourth quarter, Donahue relied upon a continuous series of fullback dive plays behind center Boozer Pitts to go almost 70 yards for a score. The starting fullback, Red Harris, had been run to exhaustion and so Donahue replaced him with Paul Bidez as the Tigers started from their own thirty-two yard line.

With Bidez fresh off the bench, Donahue called the fullback dive play again and again and again. Bidez carried the ball eleven straight times for 65 yards. Then Newell raced wide around Vanderbilt's gasping defense for a touchdown and Ted Arnold kicked the extra point to give the 14 - 6 final score and put an exclamation point on Auburn's victory. The story of the game in the *Birmingham News* was colorfully titled: "Auburn's Tigers Come From Their Lair and Viciously Claw and Tear the Flesh of Dan McGugin's Commodores." While the Auburn students and fans celebrated the win, Donahue and his team knew that another great challenge lay just ahead.

On November 22, Thanksgiving Day, Auburn faced Georgia and its senior halfback Bob McWhorter in Atlanta's Ponce De Leon Park in front of 10,000 fans and with the SIAA championship at stake. Georgia's offense relied upon McWhorter, a four-time All-Southern selection who stood only five feet nine inches tall, but who weighed 190 pounds and combined speed with power and strength. McWhorter was outstanding in 1913 and was the only Southern player named an All-American. He was Georgia's and the South's first All-American, a Herschel Walker of his day.

With the Auburn defense concentrating on stopping McWhorter on the ground, Georgia scored in the first quarter with a 30 yard touchdown pass from Dave Paddock to Harry Logan. It would be the only pass they completed, yet in a close game the touchdown could have been enough for a Georgia victory. But this game would not be close.

With a powerful offensive line and several great runners, Donahue never had Ted Arnold attempt a pass and Auburn ground out a running touchdown on a fullback dive play in each of the remaining three quarters. Red Harris scored one touchdown, while Bill Christopher scored twice to give Auburn a 21 - 7 victory over a strong Georgia team that would finish its season 6 - 2. Although halfback Kirk Newell was kept from the end zone, he ran for 121 yards, while the more celebrated runner Bob McWhorter was held to merely 50 yards by Auburn's swarming defense. When the game ended, Auburn students rushed the field and carried the Tiger players off on their shoulders, singing "Glory, glory, dear old Auburn."

Auburn completed the 1913 season undefeated, going 8 – 0, and winning the SIAA Championship again. The 1913 Auburn Tigers outscored their opponents 224 - 13 while playing the most difficult schedule of any SIAA team. They were clearly the most dominant team in the South and it was selected as national champion for 1913 by six recognized selectors. Six of Auburn's eight opponents finished with winning records, and for two of those teams, LSU and Mississippi State, the Auburn game was their only loss. The strength of the schedule can be recognized by noting that the last five teams Auburn played (Miss. State, LSU, Georgia Tech, Vanderbilt, and Georgia) were a combined 30-4-3 when not playing Auburn, and had a 29 – 3 - 1 record when not playing Auburn or each other. With six All-Southern players and led by star halfback Kirk Newell (who should have been named an All-American), the 1913 team is plainly deserving of the title of national champion for 1913.

The other teams selected as national champions for 1913 were Harvard (9 - 0) and the University of Chicago (7 – 0). While Auburn again played almost all its games on the road, Harvard played what was considered for it an "easy" schedule and had all but one game at home. In its only away game, Harvard only won a narrow 3 - 0 victory over a Princeton squad that featured former Auburn fullback Bill Streit. The University of Chicago, playing in what is now called the Big Ten Conference, only had two games away from home. While each of these teams have a valid claim to a national championship, neither has a stronger claim to the 1913 national championship than Auburn.

In sum, Auburn is a national champion for 1913 because the team was undefeated in the SIAA; shut out six of its eight opponents; played the most difficult schedule in the South, with most of games played away from home and still outscored its opponents 224 - 13; is recognized as a national champion for 1913 by the NCAA, and was chosen as national champion by six recognized selectors, James Howell's Power Ratings System, the Billingsley Report, the Hatch Mathematical College Football Rankings, 1st-N-Goal, the Dolphin Historical College Football Rankings, and the College Football Rankings of Kyle Matschke. The undefeated 1913 Auburn team, SIAA champion, is deserving of the title of national champion and that championship should be claimed by Auburn's Athletic Department with a banner in Jordan-Hare Stadium.

4

THE 1914 NATIONAL CHAMPIONSHIP SEASON

Mike Donahue's 1914 team had lost several star players to graduation and so he had to shuffle his lineup. Ted Arnold was moved from quarterback to left halfback to try and replace Kirk Newell's speed and running ability. He was replaced at quarterback by Legare "Lucy" Hairston. With "Red" Harris returning at fullback, Frank Hart was moved from fullback to right halfback, and Richard "Bull" Kearley was moved from halfback to end. Center John "Boozer" Pitts, voted an All-Southern player for the third year, anchored the line. Pitts would later be an assistant to Donahue and then replace him as head coach in 1923.

In 1914, Auburn stretched its undefeated streak to seventeen games with an 8 – 0 - 1 season that included a win over a national power, the Carlisle Indian Industrial School. The Carlisle team was composed of the native Americans of various tribes who had been sent by the government to the boarding school for an education. Certain selectors have named Carlisle the national champion for 1912, when they were led by the great All-American Jim Thorpe. In 1914, Carlisle was led by another All-American, fullback Pete Calac. With a win over Carlisle and strong SIAA teams, selector James Howell, using his Power Ratings Formula, later named the 1914 Auburn team a national champion.

Membership of the SIAA had changed again and included Alabama, Auburn, Centre, Chattanooga, Citadel, Clemson, Florida, Georgia, Howard (Samford), Kentucky, LSU, Memphis, Mercer, Mississippi , Miss. State., Sewanee, Tennessee, Texas A&M, Tulane, Vanderbilt, and Virginia.

Auburn opened the season on September 26 with a "warm-up" game against Marion Military Institute. It was expected that Auburn would win easily and so, by agreement, the length of each quarter was reduced from fifteen to only eight minutes. Despite playing barely more than what would be half of a normal game, Auburn still earned a runaway 39 - 0 victory. Red Harris and F.H. Pendergrast each had two touchdown runs.

On October 3, Auburn dispatched Hamilton Agriculture School by a 60 – 0 score. "Red" Harris and Ted Arnold each scored three touchdowns

After two games at home, Auburn traveled two days by train to Jacksonville, Florida to play the University of Florida on October 10. Playing two outmatched opponents hadn't quite prepared Auburn for a strong Florida team that would finish its season with a 5 – 2 record. Both teams played sloppy in the first half, which produced fumbles and interceptions from each side, but no points. However, Auburn finally took control of the game in the second half when halfback Frank Hart scored from the five yard line. Backup fullback Paul Bidez, hero of the prior year's Vanderbilt game, added two short touchdown runs in the fourth quarter as Florida's defense wore down and Auburn took home a 20 – 0 victory.

Auburn played its third home game on October 17 when it hosted Clemson. Auburn dominated the game from the start, scoring a touchdown when Bill Louiselle blocked a punt and George Taylor recovered it in the Clemson end zone. Auburn added a three more touchdowns, one each by "Lucy" Hairston, "Red" Harris, and Paul Bidez, to win 28 - 0 over a Clemson team that would finish 5 – 3 - 1.

Next up for Auburn in its final home game on October 24 was a strong Mississippi State team. The first quarter was scoreless defensive struggle and so Donahue went to the pass to stretch the defense. He moved Ted Arnold back to quarterback and Arnold threw a 35 yard touchdown pass to end George Steed to give Auburn had all the points it would need for a victory. F.H. Pendegrast and Paul Bidez added touchdown runs and Auburn earned a 19 – 0 victory against a Mississippi State team that would finish 6 – 2 - 1.

After a week off, Auburn traveled to Atlanta on November 7 to meet John Heisman's Georgia Tech team. Auburn players wore numbered jerseys for the first time in this game. Auburn's defense stifled Tech at every turn, causing three fumbles that were all recovered by end "Bull" Kearley. One of Kearley's fumble recoveries led directly to a score, as F.H. Pendergrast powered into the Tech end zone on a 10 yard run. Fullback Paul Bidez later scored on a short fourth-quarter run and Auburn won 14 - 0. Georgia Tech would go on to finish the season 6 – 2 - 1.

On November 14, Auburn traveled to Birmingham to play Vanderbilt at Rickwood Field before 10,000 fans. The game was played on a rain-soaked, muddy field. Auburn scored midway through the first quarter when Red Harris ran it in from the eight yard line. After that, both teams had trouble moving the football as the field conditions worsened. The Auburn defense preserved the win, stopping Vanderbilt drives on fourth down three times during the fourth quarter. The 6 - 0 victory brought Auburn's record to 7 - 0.

On November 21, Auburn traveled again to Atlanta to play the University of Georgia. Like Auburn's last game, this was a defensive struggle. Neither team could generate much offense. Georgia had had two scoring opportunities, but in each instance Auburn defenders forced and recovered fumbles to end the threats. Auburn's only scoring threat ended when a runner was tackled on the Georgia 15 yard line as time expired. The game ended in a scoreless tie.

Auburn's final game of the 1914 season was played in Atlanta at Grant Field on December 9 against the Carlisle Indian Industrial School and it generated the same excitement as a post-season bowl game. It was the first intersectional college football game played in Atlanta and was attended by Georgia's governor. Carlisle, a recognized national power, was coached by Glenn "Pop" Warner. Warner's teams were known for a high-powered offense featuring trickery and daring plays. The team was led by All-American fullback Pete Calac, who was an imposing figure as a runner at five-feet ten-inches tall and weighing 190 pounds. Calac would go on to play professional football with Jim Thorpe for the Canton Bulldogs and other teams over a ten-year career. Though Auburn was recognized as the best team in the South, Carlisle was used to playing powerful Eastern teams and had a record of 34 – 4 in the previous three seasons. Carlisle had just beaten the University of Alabama 20 - 3 in Birmingham using its second team and without its trick plays, and the mighty Calac declared that Carlisle would beat Auburn handily.

While Carlisle was favored by sportswriters, Warner found his team struggling against Auburn's strong and aggressive defense that was in the backfield before the plays could develop. In a game described as a "bitter fight" where the "battle ebbed and flowed," Auburn could not move the ball well either and the game remained a scoreless struggle until the fourth quarter. As the end of the game neared, after a series of "line plunges" that moved the ball into Carlisle territory, quarterback Lucy Hairston set up a score with a pass to halfback Richard Kearly that took the ball to Carlisle's six yard line. Then Hairston scored himself on a short scamper to give Auburn a 7 - 0 victory. Frank Hart's interception of a Carlisle pass preserved the victory.

The win over the Carlisle Indians capped off an 8 – 0 – 1 season where Auburn's defense did not surrender a single point and was the only college team to do so that year, outscored its opponents 193 – 0, and stretched its undefeated streak to seventeen games. Auburn dominated its opponents with a truly smothering defense. While Auburn finished 5 – 0 – 1 in the S.I.A.A., the conference championship was awarded to the University of Tennessee based on its 5 – 0 record. However, with Auburn having played a more difficult schedule, including the Eastern power Carlisle, several newspapers named Auburn the Champion of the South.

At season's end, team manager Jonathan Bell Lovelace wrote: "The season of 1914 is over. Auburn has humbled her opponents in her own state of Alabama, she has trampled over the bodies of the representatives of Florida, and shattered the hopes of the team from South Carolina; she has romped over the team from Mississippi A&M, shut out the candidates from the Cracker State, made the Commodores bite the dust, and defeated the invaders from the North; AND STILL HER GOAL LINE HAS NOT BEEN CROSSED.

The other teams selected as national champions for 1914 are Army (9 – 0) and the University of Illinois (7 – 0). While Army played five teams with winning records, all but one of its games was played at its home field in West Point. One of those "winning" teams, Springfield College (6 – 3) simply was not very good and posted a winning record simply because it played other lesser teams, and would be described today as a "creampuff." Likewise, Illinois played only five winning teams, three of them at home, and its victory against the Christian Brothers School (7 – 2) was another over a lesser team.

Thus, in reality, factoring out each team's single "creampuff" victory, it can be said that Army and Illinois truly only defeated four teams with winning records. Auburn matched both Army and Illinois by defeating four winning teams, but had only two of those games at home, and also defeated the Carlisle Indians who were led by All-American Pete Calac and had been favored by thirty points. The victory over Carlisle must certainly be considered as yet another quality win. Thus, Auburn was certainly the equal of both Army and Illinois in 1914.

In sum, Auburn is a national champion for 1914 because the team was undefeated; shut out all of its opponents; outscored its opponents 193 – 0 even though it played most of its games away from home; and was chosen as national champion by James Howell's Power Ratings System, a recognized selector. The 1914 Auburn team is deserving of the title of national champion and that championship should be claimed by Auburn's Athletic Department with a banner in Jordan-Hare Stadium.

5

THE POST-DONAHUE ERA: WHEN AUBURN FOOTBALL LOST ITS WAY

The undefeated streak of seventeen games during Auburn's 1913 and 1914 National Championship seasons was extended to twenty-three when the 1915 team opened the season with six straight wins. However, Auburn had graduated most of the starters of the prior two years and the inexperienced 1915 team ended the season with two losses to finish 6 - 2. The highlight of the season was Auburn's dominating 12 - 0 win over Georgia in Athens, that sportswriter O.B. Keeler called "the maddest, wildest, craziest, fightingest, grandest game of football I ever saw or ever expect to see if I live to be 80."

Coach Donahue's 1916 and 1917 teams equaled the 6-2 record, with the 1917 team adding a scoreless tie with Ohio State in a special intersectional game for Ohio troops training for WWI at Camp Sheridan, just north of Montgomery. Ohio State, led by three-time All-American runner Chic Harley, was a 30 point favorite. However, Harley was knocked out of the game early in the second half and Auburn fought the Buckeyes to a scoreless tie before a "monster crowd" of 10,000 spectators that included Ohio's governor. Harley is considered one of the best college players of the first half of the 20th Century, as in

1950 he was voted first-team on the All-Half Century team (along with Jim Thorpe and ahead of Red Grange). In his career, Ohio State went 21 – 1 – 1, and in 1917, it was 8 – 0 – 1 and Big Ten Champion. Thus, in one of the all-time classic games of Auburn football, the 1917 team showed that Auburn's program was the equal of the Northern elite.

After fielding no team during the World War I year of 1918, Auburn's football program rose to prominence again with an 8 – 1 record (a one-point loss to Vanderbilt in Nashville) and another SIAA Championship in 1919. It was a season for which retroactive selectors have ranked Auburn as high as second nationally and was thus almost another national championship season. The next two years Auburn went only 12 – 5, but then rebounded with an 8 – 2 record in 1922, the initial year of the Southern Conference.

But during the 1922 season rumors began that Coach Donahue was going to resign at season's end. Newspapers reported that members of the Klu Klux Klan in the Alabama Legislature threatened to cut Auburn's funding unless Donahue, a Catholic, was removed from such an important position. Auburn supported Donahue in the face of the Klan's growing political power and refused to bow to the pressure. But late in the season the players began to suspect the rumors were indeed true. Just before a game in front of 17,000 fans in Birmingham against a then powerful Centre College team led by three All-Americans, Donahue exhorted his team not to "fight and win for Auburn," as he had always done, but instead, with emotions barely contained, he pleaded, "For the first time today, I'm asking you to go out and win this one for Mike." And that they did, winning 6 – 0 against a Centre College team whose only other loss was in a close game with Harvard played in

Boston. In true Donahue fashion, Auburn won with defense on a blocked punt recovered for a touchdown.

Two days before the final game at Georgia Tech, a Birmingham newspaper reported that Donahue had tendered his resignation letter to Auburn President Spright Dowell. However, by the day of the game, Donahue was talked out of resigning. Yet a month later, Donahue changed his mind again.

When Dowell became Auburn's President in 1920, he brought an anti-college football morality with him to the position. He immediately took actions to undercut the strength and popularity of the sports program, making Donahue's difficult job as head coach of the football, basketball, and baseball programs, even harder. Donahue had been worn down by 19 years of hard work coaching football at a small college with little natural resources for a winning program, and where the prospects for continued success were waning because of Dowell's restrictions and financial cuts. Facing threats from the Klan, Donahue must simply have wanted a fresh start elsewhere. Louisiana State University provided that, along with a Catholic community in Baton Rouge. In 1923, he signed a five-year contract with LSU for a $10,000 salary, nearly doubling the $5200 he had been paid by Auburn, and four times the sum LSU had paid his predecessor. Unfortunately for LSU, spending the most money on a football coach of any Southern Conference school could not guarantee championships. The magic Donahue had worked at Auburn was not repeated and his record at LSU before turning down a contract renewal and resigning was only 28 – 19 – 3.

Through 19 years, Mike Donahue and Auburn football had been inseparable. After another SIAA championship in 1919 and a near miss in 1922, it was expected that Auburn would win more championships in the 1920's with Donahue in charge. After all, he had been hired in 1904 at age 25 and was still in his forties, with possibly two decades left to coach. He had taken "green" farm boys and built a football power that had raised Auburn's national profile by playing intersectional games against Texas, Texas A&M, Navy, Carlisle, and Ohio State. But then, with his unexpected resignation, Auburn's early championship era suddenly came to a close.

Auburn officials weren't prepared for having to find a replacement for Donahue; they had hardly considered the possibility. Nor had they spent much time thinking about the Auburn football program in general. That was Donahue's to worry about. President Dowell disliked college athletics and, with the college's funding strained, he had little interest in finding a strong replacement, even though under Donahue's leadership the athletic program was profitable.

Auburn's leadership failed to realize what other colleges and universities were beginning to understand – that athletic programs could be used as a means to attract more students and thus expand campus facilities. For example, across the state at the University of Alabama, President Denny placed a new emphasis on the football program in the 1920's. Alabama also found itself having to find a new head football coach in 1922 after Xen Scott was diagnosed with cancer. Denny hired Wallace Wade, Dan McGugin's top assistant at powerful Vanderbilt, and used the successes of Wade's teams to gain notoriety outside the South and attract out-of-state students. With the Alabama President Denny's emphasis on the football program and the President Dowell's disdain for the Auburn program, in the critical year of 1922 the paths of the two programs diverged for three decades. At Alabama, football had become the priority. In 1925, Governor William Brandon, a Tuscaloosa native, personally lobbied for Alabama to be chosen to play in the 1926 Rose Bowl, and when Tulane turned down the invitation for academic reasons, Alabama was offered and eagerly accepted. With a 20 - 19 win over Washington in the Rose Bowl, the Alabama program, inferior to Auburn's for three decades, suddenly became nationally acclaimed at a time when Auburn's program hit new lows because of President Dowell's restrictions.

While other Southern schools such as Alabama began offering "student service payments" (i.e., athletic scholarships) and otherwise recruiting star players from distant locations, Auburn was still using Donahue's "class team" intramural system to develop ordinary students into football players and would continue to do so for years to come. Home games were still being played at Drake Field (at the location of Haley Center and the Student Union) where spectators sat on aging wooden bleachers.

However, Auburn's competitors had been planning ahead. Georgia Tech had constructed Grant Field in 1913 with wooden grandstands that could seat almost 6,000 fans. By the time Donahue left Auburn for LSU, Grant Field was in the process of expanding to seat 30,000 people. At Vanderbilt, Auburn's other challenger for early dominance in football in the South, 1922 saw the completion of Dudley Field, which could seat 20,000 spectators and was the first football-only stadium in the South. At LSU, Tiger Stadium was under construction when Donahue arrived as the new head coach and it seated 12,000 when it opened in 1924.

Across the state from Auburn, Alabama was planning the construction of an on-campus stadium, and by the end of the decade Denny Stadium opened with a capacity of 12,000 spectators.

However, there were no plans for a stadium at Auburn in 1922. Nor would there be for many years to come. And there was no plan for replacing arguably the greatest coach in Auburn's 120 years of football history. President Dowell made the decision to simply hire one of Donahue's assistants, be done with it, and get back to the business of education and research. And so, one of the stars of the 1913 team and Team Captain of the 1914 squad, John "Boozer" Pitts, was hired as Auburn's new head football coach. But Pitts, though an All-Southern selection as a center in both 1913 and 1914, was wholly unprepared to be the head coach of a college football team.

Then a mathematics professor at Auburn, Pitts was only nominally a football coach under Donahue. His duties had consisted of being a "scout" who attended the game of Auburn's upcoming opponent to determine the team's strengths and weaknesses. He was nearly a decade removed from the day-to-day operations of a college football program, which had changed dramatically in the years since he had played. In hiring Pitts, who did not have any offensive or defensive systems of his own or even any experience coaching even one game, the future of Auburn football was left to whatever momentum would be left over from the Donahue years.

That momentum waned quickly and what would follow was a mostly dismal period of coaching musical chairs that would last for three decades until Ralph "Shug" Jordan was hired in 1951. Pitts led Auburn to a 3 – 3 – 3 record in 1923, a 4 – 4 -1 record in 1924, and then stepped down to resume teaching duties fulltime. He was replaced by Dave Morey, a fast-talking Yankee who had been the head coach at Middlebury College in Vermont. The reason Auburn officials chose Morey to be the next head football coach is probably lost to the passage of time. Morey produced a 5 – 3 – 1 record in 1925 that included wins over both Vanderbilt and Virginia Tech, and a tie with Georgia Tech, but blowout losses to Georgia and Texas. The 1926 season produced a similar 5 – 4 result, but included three straight losses to end the season that showed signs of what was to come in 1927. After three losses to start that season, Morey resigned, Boozer Pitts had to step in as head coach to finish the season, and Auburn's football program was in a state of collapse. Just five years after Coach Donahue had resigned, Auburn failed to win a game and struggled to a 0-7-2 record that ultimately cost President Dowell his job.

Auburn then hired Southerner George Bohler as its next head football coach. He had coached Mississippi College and produced an impressive 17 – 3 record the prior two years. Alumni hoped for a quick improvement in the team. But Bohler was unprepared for coaching against the stronger programs of the Southern Conference, and he had no bag of tricks to work immediate magic. After a 1 – 8 season in 1928, and a 1 – 4 start in 1929, Bohler was fired, an assistant took over as the interim coach, and the team did not win another game that season.

With the Auburn football program at a dismal 2 – 23 – 1 record over the previous three seasons, the Auburn administration finally made a good hire in choosing Chet Wynne to be Auburn's next head coach. Wynne had played fullback for Knute Rockne at Notre Dame, had played professional football, and had just finished his seventh year as the head coach at Creighton University. Wynne had quite a rebuilding job to do and the first thing he did was scrap the Line-Divide offensive formation originated by Donahue two decades earlier that was still being used. In its place he instituted use of the more modern "Notre Dame box" formation, a variant of the "single wing" that was popular in that era. Using Wynn's new systems, the team improved to a 3 – 7 record in 1930, which was taken as a sign of improvement. A 5 – 3 record followed in 1931, the first truly "winning" season in nearly a decade.

A halfback named Jimmy Hitchcock had begun to make a name for himself during the 1930 and 1931 seasons. But the college football world didn't expect what happened in 1932. In his senior season, Hitchcock exploded onto that national football scene and led Wynne's squad to a 9 – 0 – 1 record and a Southern Conference championship. Hitchcock, nicknamed "the Phantom from Union Springs," was clearly Auburn's best player since Kirk Newell. A true triple threat player, in 1932 Hitchcock accounted for touchdowns by running the ball, passing, returning a punt, and returning a pass interception. He was also the starting punter and one of the best in college football, never having even one punt blocked in his fours years. Hitchcock led the way for Auburn's biggest victory of the year, a 19 – 7 win over Tulane, which had won the three prior Southern Conference championships, 36 of its prior 38 games, and was then considered the "Goliath of Southern football." But without do-it-all Hitchcock, Auburn's first consensus All-American, the 1933 team stumbled to a 5 – 5 record and after the season Wynne accepted an offer to be the football coach and athletic director at Kentucky, which was much closer to his Chicago home.

John "Silent Jack" Meagher, another former player of Knute Rocke's at Notre Dame, was the next coach to get his chance to turn around Auburn's football fortunes. Meagher came to Auburn from Rice University, where he'd coached the Owls to a 26 – 26 record over five years. Meagher's overall record over nine years at Auburn was 48 – 37 – 10. When World War II was declared, Meagher entered the military and ended his college coaching career.

Auburn's best years during Meagher's tenure were 1935 through 1937 when the Tigers were 21 – 6 – 2, and went to their first two bowl games. In both 1935 and 1936, contemporary selectors rated Auburn a Top Ten team nationally. It looked like Auburn football was returning to prominence, but the success of those years could not be sustained and the highlight of Auburn football during the end of Meagher's tenure was Auburn's upset of top-ranked Georgia in 1942, where the Tigers were led to victory by All-American running back Monk Gafford.

The greatest legacy of Jack Meagher as Auburn's head football coach and Athletic Director is that he managed to push the Auburn administration to agree to build an on-campus football stadium so that home games would no longer have to be played in Birmingham, Montgomery, Atlanta, and Columbus. In the absence of a home stadium and with faster train travel, Meagher scheduled games for Auburn from one end of the country to the other. In the last years of the 1930's Auburn played games as far away as San Francisco, Detroit, Philadelphia, New York (at the Polo Grounds), and Boston (at Fenway Park). But with the opening of Auburn Stadium in 1939, Auburn had finally committed to building the foundation for the type of modern football program it had been competing against for two decades. All Auburn needed was to hire the right man as head coach to build on what Jack Meagher had accomplished.

However, it took Auburn another decade to get it right. As World War II neared its end, Auburn decided to resume playing football in 1944. In mid-summer, Carl Voyles, who had led William & Mary College to a 29 - 7 - 3 record, was hired as the new head coach and Athletics Director. But Voyles' tenure was short-lived and disappointing, and he was fired after four years with a record of 17 – 22.

Wilbur Hutsell, the head coach of the track and field program and who had been involved with Auburn's football program since the early 1920's, replaced Voyles as Athletic Director. In 1948, Auburn decided to hire yet another former Notre Dame player, Earl Brown, as head football coach. Perhaps it made sense at the time in that the two coaches since Donahue who had experienced success at Auburn, Wynne and Meagher, had both played at Notre Dame.

Former Auburn lineman Ralph "Shug" Jordan, who was then an assistant to Wally Butts at Georgia, had actively campaigned for the job. But Auburn chose to hire Brown instead. He had head been the head coach at both Dartmouth and Canisius and had led both to winning records. But Brown quickly proved to be an even worse hire than Voyles. He was fired at the end of a 0 – 10 season in 1950 with an overall 3 – 22 – 4 record. Once again, Auburn football had hit rock bottom.

After 30 years in the wilderness, it was time to give an Auburn man the chance to lead Auburn's football program.

6

COACH RALPH "SHUG" JORDAN AND THE 1958 NATIONAL CHAMPIONSHIP SEASON

Given Ralph "Shug" Jordan's status as a legend at Auburn, where he was head coach for 25 years, it is easy to assume that he was destined to get that job. However, it almost didn't happen. Although Jordan had campaigned for the Auburn head coaching job in 1948, the administration chose Earl Brown, yet another former Notre Dame player. When the job came open again in 1951 when Brown was fired, Jordan wasn't interested in getting turned down once more by his alma mater. He had given much of his life to Auburn, as a student and player under Coaches Bohler and Wynne; as an assistant coach and then head coach of he freshmen team under Coaches Wynne and Meagher from 1932 to 1937; as a varsity coach in charge of the centers under Coach Meagher from 1938 to 1942; and, after serving in combat in World War II, as an assistant coach under Coach Voyles before crossing state lines to join Coach Butts' staff at Georgia in 1946. When he applied for the job in 1948 and wasn't chosen, Jordan focused his mind on his job at Georgia and possible coaching jobs elsewhere.

But shortly after Coach Brown was fired at Auburn, Wilbur Hutsell stepped down as Auburn's Athletic Director to focus on coaching the track and field program and to allow for his replacement as Athletic Director, Jeff Beard, who had been the Athletic Department's business manager, to run the search for the new football coach. Beard, who had known Jordan since their boyhoods, had only one man in mind for the job. But first he had to convince Jordan to apply for the job, and Beard knew that because of Shug's stubbornness, it wasn't going to be easy. Eventually, he Jordan agreed to write a letter to the members of the search committee.

But with over 200 coaches applying for the position, Jordan didn't make Beard's job of consolidating support around him an easy one. Rather than detail in the letter how he would go about bringing Auburn football back to its winning tradition, Jordan simply wrote: "I hereby apply for the head coaching job at Auburn. Sincerely, Ralph Jordan." The search committee reduced the applicants to Jordan and three others. Then, by a 3 – 2 vote, Jordan was chosen over LSU line coach, Norm Cooper. When Shug was announced as Auburn's head coach on February 26, 1951, Auburn's journey back to winning championships had taken its first step.

When Mike Donahue took over as Auburn's head coach in 1904, he produced an immediately improved team that finished 7 – 0, but then suffered two losing seasons before he had the foundation of a winning program in place. In Jordan's first year, the returning players from the squad that had gone 0 – 10 started out an amazing 5 – 1, only to fade to 5 – 5. Then in 1952, the record fell to 2 – 8 and doubts began to creep into the Auburn faithful. But in 1953, Jordan led Auburn to a 7 – 3 – 1 record, the first bowl game since the 1938 Orange Bowl, and a number seventeen ranking the Associated Press poll.

The 1954 season proved the prior year's success was not a fluke and that Auburn was once again ready to compete for championships. Auburn started out slowly in 1954, losing three of its first four games. But Jordan made some changes in his starting lineup and the team then won seven straight and finished the season with whippings of Georgia (35 – 0), Clemson (27 – 6), Alabama (28 – 0), and Baylor (33 – 13) in a Gator Bowl victory to finish the season. The eleven starters in those last seven games of 1954 (who played both ways) are thought by some to be Auburn's best team ever. With a final ranking of 13th in the 1954 A.P. poll and confidence in Coach Jordan, Auburn had added 13,000 seats to Cliff Hare Stadium for the 1955 season, raising capacity to almost 35,000 seats.

That confidence was well placed as in 1955 Jordan led Auburn to an 8 – 2 – 1 record, another Gator Bowl, and a top ten finish in the A.P. poll. Auburn stumbled to start the 1956 season, but as in 1954, the team finished with a flourish, winning four straight games that included whippings of rivals Georgia (20 – 0) and Alabama (34 – 7) to finish 7 – 3. Some of the star players at Auburn during those first years of Jordan's coaching tenure are now legendary names to Auburn fans: quarterback Vince Dooley, All-American receiver Jim Pyburn, All-American receiver Jimmy Phillips, All-SEC fullback Joe Childress, All-American offensive tackle Frank D'Agostino, and All-American running back Fob James

No one needs a reminder about the great success of Auburn's 1957 season, where Coach Jordan's efforts to rebuild Auburn into a national championship team came to fruition. In less than a decade, Shug Jordan had taken a team that had gone 0 – 10 in 1950 and turned it into a 10 – 0

Southeastern Conference champion that was the runaway winner of the national championship vote by the poll taken of the 360 sportswriters of the Associated Press. Second place in the Associated Press Poll went to an Ohio State team that finished 9 – 1 and had struggled to beat an unranked Oregon team in the Rose Bowl by a 10 – 7 score, but was named a national champion by the U.P.I. poll.

Auburn's 1957 national championship was won based on a rock-hard defense that allowed only 28 points all season and was statistically the strongest in the nation. The defense was led by players such as Zeke Smith, and even Iron Mike Donahue (who was then still alive) would have been proud of and the team's aggressive play. In addition to the Associated Press, Auburn has been named the 1957 national champion by numerous other recognized selectors, including, but not limited to the Billingsley Report, the Massey Ratings of Kenneth Massey, Nutshell Sports Football Ratings, James Howell's Power Ratings System, the Helms Athletic Foundation, and the National Championship Foundation.

With four straight wins to end the 1956 season and ten wins in the undefeated 1957 national championship season, Auburn started the 1958 season with a fourteen game winning streak. In 1958, as in 1957, the SEC had twelve member teams: Auburn, Alabama, Florida, Georgia, Georgia Tech, Kentucky, LSU, Mississippi, Mississippi State, Tennessee, Tulane, and Vanderbilt. In that era, SEC teams played only a six or seven game SEC schedule and thus did not play all of their conference foes.

Auburn lost quite a few starters from the 1957 team, but many star players returned for the 1958 season, including quarterback Lloyd Nix, All-SEC end Jerry Wilson,

All-American receiver Jimmy Phillips, All-American and Outland award winning lineman Zeke Smith, All-American center Jackie Burkett, and All-SEC tackle Cleve Wester. Expectations for the 1958 season were sky-high and the pre-season polls ranked Auburn third. Auburn would go on to have another undefeated season, finishing 9 – 0 – 1, lead the nation in total defense, and be named national champion by the selector Montgomery Full Season Championship, which named annual national champions for 1936 through 1982.

As it had done for the prior few seasons, Auburn opened the 1958 season with a game against Tennessee on September 27. The 44,000 fans at Legion Field in Birmingham and the nationwide television audience were shown a display from Auburn on how to play defense. Not only did Tennessee fail to make a single first down the entire game, the Volunteers gained only 19 yards passing and lost 49 yards on running plays. Thus, for the game, Tennessee was held to a minus thirty yards of offense. Auburn had not been a powerhouse on offense in 1957, but didn't need to be given its nation's best defense. With capable runner Lloyd Nix at quarterback, Auburn ran an offense that often gave him a run or pass option. Auburn scored twice in the second half and that was enough for the win. Halfback Lamar Rawson powered into the end zone score from the four yard line and then halfback Tommy Lorino scored on a 24 yard run and to cap off a 13 – 0 victory.

After the victory against a tough Tennessee team, Auburn experienced a bit of a let down during its October 4 game against Chattanooga. Auburn led only 6 – 0 at the half on a 48 yard pass from backup quarterback Johnny Kern to Jimmy Laster. In the second half, sophomore back Ed Dyas, who would be named an All-American in 1960 and finish fourth in balloting for the Heisman Trophy that year, showed his great potential with an exciting 62 yard run for another score. Chattanooga scored on a pass play after a long kickoff return brought the ball back to near the Tigers' goal line. However, Auburn's aggressive defense then shut down Chattanooga offense and the Tigers put the game away with three successive touchdowns. Quarterbacks Lloyd Nix and Richard Wood both scored on short runs, and a long Nix to Laster pass for a touchdown ended the scoring for a 30 – 8 Auburn victory.

On October 11, Auburn traveled to Lexington to play the University of Kentucky before a capacity crowd of 36,000. The game was a scoreless defensive struggle through the first three quarters. But early in the fourth quarter, Lloyd Nix hit Jimmy Laster with a 43 yard scoring strike for a 6 - 0 lead. Then Zeke Smith tackled a Kentucky runner in its own end zone for a safety and Auburn had a hard-fought 8 – 0 victory.

On October 18, Auburn traveled to Atlanta to play Georgia Tech before a capacity crowd at Grant Field. Auburn scored first on a short second quarter touchdown run by Ed Dyas for a 7 – 0 lead. Auburn's defense did its part, holding Tech to just 58 yards rushing, but Auburn's offense, while gaining over 230 yards rushing, couldn't manage another score. In the fourth quarter, a Tech player intercepted a pass, ran it back to Auburn's 36 yard line, and then Tech capitalized with a touchdown to tie the game. The final score was 7 – 7 and, though Auburn dominated statistically, the winning streak was snapped. But give that the game was a tie and not a loss, Auburn's streak of being undefeated extended to 18 games.

Auburn next played Maryland at home in Cliff Hare Stadium. In the second quarter, Lamar Rawson intercepted a pass and returned it to Maryland's 12 yard line. That set up a short touchdown pass from Johnny Kern, who was playing for injured starter Lloyd Nix, to halfback Tommy Lorino. In the third quarter, Jim Reynolds ran for a 62 yard score and Maryland responded with their own long pass play for a score. But Auburn clinched the 20 – 7 win when Tommy Lorino, playing both ways as players did in that era, intercepted a pass and returned it to the Maryland 20 yard line and then added his second touchdown of the game on a short run.

The November 5 game against the University of Florida in Gainesville was another defensive struggle. Florida fielded a defense as strong as Auburn's and both teams knew a single touchdown could be enough for a win. The first half ended in a scoreless tie. Then in the third, Florida went ahead 3 – 0 on a 32 yard field goal, and it looked like that lead might hold. But in the fourth quarter, Lloyd Nix started a drive that mixed in several passes and moved the ball to Florida's side of the field. Believing the Gator's secondary was vulnerable, Jordan substituted Richard Wood, a more accurate passer, for Nix. Wood then completed two passes, including a touchdown pass to Joe Leichtman from the 10 yard line. Wood also made a key play to preserve the lead. Florida's Dave Hudson took off on a long run and it looked like he would score, but Wood, also playing safety, knocked him out of bounds at the three yard line. Zeke Smith caused a Florida fumbled on the next play and Auburn recovered, ending Florida's scoring threat. Leading only 6 – 3 and pinned back against its goal line as the game neared its end, Auburn purposefully took a safety instead of risking having a punt blocked and to be able to kick from the 20 yard line. Florida was unable to move the ball, was too far out to try a winning field goal, and Auburn preserved a 6 – 5 road game victory.

Auburn returned home to play Mississippi State University on November 8. Auburn's offense and the passing game finally got rolling with Richard Wood at quarterback from the start. Wood led Auburn to three first-half scores, including two touchdown passes to Jimmy Pettus and a seven yard run of his own for a touchdown. State capitalized on Auburn miscues in the second quarter, when a long punt return and recovery of an Auburn fumble set up short touchdown drives. However, Auburn put the game away in the second half when Loyd Nix took over quarterbacking duties. Nix threw a long touchdown pass of his own to Pettus and then scored himself on a 13 yard run that finished off a clock-eating drive. In the 33 – 14 win over Mississippi State, Auburn showed that it finally had a passing game to complement its power running attack.

Up next for Auburn on November 15 was a game against its longtime rival, the University of Georgia, played in Columbus, Georgia for the last time. After a scoreless first quarter, Auburn's offense got on track and built a 21 – 0 lead. A 44 yard pass from Richard Wood to Bobby Lauder capped an 80 yard drive. Lloyd Nix then came in to quarterback and led a drive that ended with a touchdown pass to Ed Dyas. After Wood intercepted a Fran Tarkenton pass, Lauder scored again on a sweep. Georgia finally scored late in the fourth quarter to escape a shutout and the final score was 21 – 6.

Wake Forest University traveled to Auburn for a game on November 22. Auburn scored in the first quarter when Ed Dyas returned an interception for a touchdown, but the Demon Deacons tied the game when they had a long scoring drive in the second quarter. Auburn took the lead in the third quarter when Lloyd Nix led a long drive that ended when he kept the ball on a short touchdown run. Auburn added another touchdown in the fourth quarter on a 33 yard run by Tommy Lorino to bring the final score to 21 – 7.

Next up for Auburn, which had moved to number two in the polls, was a game in Birmingham at Legion Field against its arch-rival, the University of Alabama, on November 29. Auburn had defeated Alabama the prior year in a 40 – 0 rout, but Alabama had hired Paul "Bear" Bryant away from Texas A&M to rebuild its program and Bryant fielded a much stronger team. Auburn took a 7 – 0 lead in the first quarter when Richard Wood led a drive that ended with a short touchdown pass to Jimmy Pettus. That score held through halftime and into the fourth quarter until Jim Reynolds capped a scoring drive with a one yard plunge and Auburn extended its lead to 14 – 0. Later in the fourth quarter Alabama scored a rushing touchdown and made a two-point conversion to bring the score to 14 – 8. Alabama then tried an onside kickoff, but Auburn caught the ball and was able to run out the clock for a fifth victory in a row against the Crimson Tide and an undefeated streak of twenty-four games.

Auburn, 9 – 0 – 1, was chosen as a national champion for 1958 by the recognized selector Montgomery Full Season Championship system, created by David Montgomery, who used a mathematic formula to determine national champions for the seasons from 1936 to 1982. Other teams recognized as national champions for 1958 are LSU (11 – 0) and the University of Iowa (8 – 1 – 1). However, Auburn, a defending 1957 national champion, was just as deserving as being recognized as a national champion for 1958.

LSU was chosen as a national champion by almost every selector, yet a review of the facts shows that Auburn's season was the plainly the equal of LSU's. Auburn's defense was dominant, as the Tigers led the conference and the nation in fewest yards allowed per game. But the offense was also productive as it led the conference in total yards gained per game. LSU's record in the SEC was 6 – 0, while Auburn played an additional conference game and also went undefeated at 6 – 0 – 1. The SEC was a very balanced league in 1958 and the two best teams, Auburn and LSU, didn't play each other.

Perhaps the best comparison of the two teams is to examine their SEC opponents to determine their strength of schedule. The SEC record of LSU's six conference opponents was 14 – 25 – 3, while the record of Auburn's seven conference opponents was slightly stronger at 17 – 26 – 4. Neither was LSU's out-of-conference schedule more difficult than Auburn's. LSU played Rice, Miami (which was only 2 – 8 that season), Duke, and Hardin-Simmons (now a D-III team). Auburn's three out-of-conference opponents were Wake Forest, Maryland, and University of Tennessee-Chattanooga. Given equivalent schedules, it would seem the only reason LSU was chosen as national champion is that, with the benefit of a slightly easier schedule, it won every game it played while Auburn, the defending national champion, had one tie. In truth, though, the quality of Auburn's 1958 season was equivalent to LSU's and the only way to demonstrate that one was the better team was if they could have played on a neutral field.

The other team chosen as national champion in 1958 was Iowa. Though Iowa played a more difficult schedule than either LSU or Auburn, it did not finish that schedule unscathed. Iowa tied Air Force and lost to Ohio State to finish 8 – 1 – 1. It was chosen as national champion by only one selector, the Football Writers Association of America. With the nation's best defense and a capable offense, the 1958 Auburn Tigers certainly had a season that was equivalent to that of LSU or Iowa.

In sum, Auburn is a national champion for 1958 because as defending National Champion the Tigers went undefeated; they dominated their opponents by shutting out two teams and only allowing one to score more than eight points; and they were chosen as national champion by the Montgomery Full Season Championship, a recognized selector. The undefeated 1958 Auburn team is deserving of the title of national champion and that championship should be claimed by Auburn's Athletic Department with a banner in Jordan-Hare Stadium.

7

THE REMAINING COACH JORDAN AND
COACH BARFIELD ERAS:
A ROLLERCOASTER RIDE

There is no doubt that Coach Jordan did a tremendous job rebuilding Auburn into a national power during the 1950's, but he could not consistently maintain that high level of success into the second and third decades of his career at Auburn. Although there were near misses at championship seasons in 1963, 1971, 1972 and 1974, those great seasons were mixed with disappointing ones.

On paper, Coach Jordan had perhaps his best team ever in 1959. The team returned four players that already had or would reach All-American status in Zeke Smith, Ken Rice, Jackie Burkett, and Ed Dyas. But in 1959 and going forward, the national championship level of success that Coach Jordan had achieved could not be replicated. Jordan would coach until 1975, and Auburn had winning teams in all but two of those years, but only five seasons after 1958 that could be called outstanding.

There are a number of factors that combined to impact Jordan's success in the latter part of his coaching career at Auburn. One factor, seen with even the greatest of coaches, is the natural ups and downs of a football program over time as assistant coaches come and go, complacency occurs and has to be replaced by new zeal for the job, and changes occur in the game itself that require adaptations that sometimes become more difficult as a head coach ages.

All these things happened with Coach Jordan, who by the early 1960's had lost many of the original assistant coaches he had relied upon. The game of college football had changed by that time to be more passing-based and he was slow to adapt from his conservative style of football that he had learned in the Thirties. The power running offense Jordan had once won so many games with -- not so much different than that run by Iron Mike Donahue's teams -- was now seen as boring and old-fashioned. Several years of probation with bowl bans had hurt recruiting, which then led to sub-par seasons that led to Auburn being no longer seen as a national power.

And the SEC competition strove to get better. Former Auburn quarterback and Jordan assistant coach Vince Dooley took over as head football coach at the University of Georgia in 1964, Doug Dickey took over at the University of Tennessee that same year, and both began winning SEC championships. But the biggest change among Auburn's competition in the Southeastern Conference is that in 1958, Paul "Bear" Bryant left Texas A&M after four years and returned to his alma mater, the University of Alabama, as head coach. Bryant, having left the Texas A&M University football program on probation, used Auburn's own probation to his advantage in recruiting and in a few short years led Alabama to its own first Associated Press National Championship and several more championships that decade. With Bryant at Alabama and Dooley at Georgia,

Jordan faced difficulty in recruiting the best players in the geographic area where Auburn had always concentrated its recruiting. So, by the time Jordan retired after the 1975 season, his successor, Coach Doug Barfield, would not be handed an easy job.

But, in 1959, Auburn was still on the top of the college football world and expectations were high. After the great success of 1957 and 1958, Auburn unexpectedly stumbled in its first game of 1959, losing 3 – 0 to Tennessee, then later losing to Georgia and Alabama for a disappointing 7 – 3 record. Auburn rebounded with a strong team in 1960 when Cliff Hare Stadium was expanded to a capacity of 45,000 seats, but narrow losses to both Tennessee (10 - 3) and Alabama (3 – 0) left Auburn with an 8 - 2 record. Auburn stumbled to 6 – 4 and 6 – 3 – 1 records in 1961 and 1962, but rebounded in 1963 with a team that featured quarterback Jimmy Sidle (who would lead the SEC in rushing) and halfback Tucker Frederickson. Auburn was once again in the national championship hunt, but a loss to the University of Nebraska in the Orange Bowl left Auburn at 9 – 2 and with a national ranking of fifth.

Given the success of the 1963 season, Auburn was once again among the nation's elite teams and Jordan believed he had a team that could indeed win the National Championship again in 1964. He was not the only one. Sports Illustrated magazine rated Auburn number one in its pre-season issue that featured Jimmy Sidle on the cover. Auburn had succeeded on offense in 1963 based largely on a quarterback roll out play where Sidle could either run or pass, and the 1964 offense was designed around the senior star, who was considered a strong Heisman Trophy candidate. However, in the opening game against the

University of Houston, Sidle was knocked out of bounds, landed hard on his shoulder, and suffered a rotator cuff tear. Though he continued to play, Sidle couldn't pass effectively and, without his passing threat, Auburn's offense was completely one-dimensional. Thus, scoring points became close to impossible for the 1964 Tigers and opponents held Auburn to the lowest season point total for any Jordan team. In an effort to spark the offense, late in the season Sidle was moved to tailback and Tucker Fredrickson to fullback. The moves were successful and resulted in a win over arch rival Georgia, but for the season Auburn's record was a disappointing 6 – 4. Thus, what had been anticipated as a dream season turned into a nightmare. After a 5 – 5 – 1 season in 1965 and an even worse 4 – 6 record in 1966, Coach Jordan was faced with heavy criticism. Some alumni believed the game had passed him by and called for him to be fired.

Jordan realized there was a desperate need to rebuild the program completely and he planned to do just that. His longtime defensive coordinator, Hal Herring, whose defenses had three times led the nation in fewest yards allowed, had moved on to the Atlanta Falcons after the 1965 season. Jordan had replaced him in 1966 with Lee Haley, but the defense had been a real weakness and so Jordan replaced Haley with Paul Davis. Jordan's offensive coordinator, Buck Bradberry, whose conservative offense had been highly ineffective in 1965, had resigned at the end of the season. He had been replaced as offensive coordinator in 1966 by receivers coach Gene Lorendo, who was eager to direct a passing offense. With Jordan finally willing to update Auburn's offensive philosophy after several sub-par seasons, there was immediate improvement in the offense in the 1967 season as quarterback Loran Carter led the SEC in total offense. Auburn finished the season with a 6 – 4 record that included a narrow and controversial loss to Alabama. The improved record in 1967 provided was some evidence that Jordan's rebuilding of the program would be successful. In 1968, Auburn finished 7 - 4, including a bowl game victory, and finished ranked seventeenth in the final polls. Jordan finally had Auburn on its way back to winning football.

During the fall signing period in 1968, Coach Jordan signed James Owens to a football scholarship. He became Auburn's first African-American football player and went on to star as a fullback for the Tigers from 1969 to 1972, a highly successful and memorable period of Auburn football. In signing Owen to a scholarship, Auburn followed Kentucky and Tennessee and became the third SEC school to integrate its football program. Owens, now a pastor, was recently honored by Auburn University, which created the James Owens Courage Award to be given to those who exemplify his courage in integrating an SEC football team during the 1960's.

By 1969, Jordan had grudgingly accepted an offense built almost completely around the passing game. And that was a good thing, because the "Sullivan to Beasley" era of 1969 to 1971 was about to begin. Quarterback Pat Sullivan and receiver Terry Beasley proved to be the greatest passing combination that the SEC had ever seen, and that probably holds true to this day given that they played together for three years. In his first year as starting quarterback, Sullivan led Auburn to a season where the offense scored more than fifty points in three games, snapped a five-game losing streak to Alabama with a 49 – 26 victory, and finished with a final record of 8 – 3.

Fans expected even more in 1970, when Cliff Hare Stadium capacity was expanded to almost 62,000 seats. They were not disappointed as the Sullivan to Beasley aerial show helped Auburn set a record for points scored in a season (390 points in 11 games) on the way to a 9 – 2 record. National attention was focused on All-American Pat Sullivan in 1971 as a Heisman Trophy candidate who was leading his team to one win after another. Following a 35 – 20 win over Georgia that brought Auburn's record to 9 – 0, Sullivan was selected the Heisman Trophy winner. The shift in focus of the team from the games ahead to celebrating Sullivan's award proved costly, as Auburn's chance at another national championship ended in consecutive losses that brought another 9 – 2 season.

Jordan had indeed succeeded in rebuilding the program with a passing offense, but with the graduation of Sullivan, Beasley, and several other stars of the last three years, there was a sense that the record of 26 – 7 over those years should have been even better. And there was concern over how Auburn was going to respond in 1972 without strong replacements at quarterback and wide-receiver for All-Americans Sullivan and Beasley.

College football prognosticators expected Auburn to be mediocre at best in 1972, but Shug Jordan was about to do the best coaching job of his career. With the heart and soul of his passing offense having graduated, Jordan brought back his two tight end, three running back offense from 1963 and worked his team through the winter and spring as hard or harder than he had worked any of his teams over the prior twenty years.

What the 1972 team lacked in star players would be made up with grit, determination, and fundamentals. And although the offense featuring quarterback Randy Walls and running back Terry Henley wasn't pretty, Auburn won games they were not expected to win against a schedule as tough as any in the country. In week three, Auburn defeated fourth-ranked University of Tennessee, 10 – 6, and ended the Vols' ten game winning streak. The next week Auburn defeated the eighteenth ranked University of Mississippi, 19 – 13, and ended the Rebels' ten game winning streak. Auburn finally came up short against eighth-ranked LSU in a night game in Baton Rouge before a record crowd in Tiger Stadium, but continued winning thereafter. Auburn beat seventeenth ranked Florida State, an undefeated Alabama team ranked second, and then the thirteenth-ranked Colorado Buffaloes in the Gator Bowl to cap off a 10 – 1 season and a final ranking of fifth. That team, "the Amazin's," will long be remembered in Auburn lore and would have been SEC champion had Alabama, who Auburn had beaten, not played an additional conference game.

In 1973, the offense struggled again, and Auburn couldn't repeat the magic formula for winning that had worked so well the year before. The Tigers stumbled to finish with a just a 6 – 6 record. In 1974, Coach Jordan brought in a new offensive coordinator, Doug Barfield, to help solve the problem. The offense featured Phil Gargis at quarterback and running backs Sedric McIntyre and Mitzi Jackson. Auburn had a powerful running attack from the new veer offense that Barfield had installed and the team finished 10 – 2, including the highlight of an exciting 24 - 3 win over Texas in the Gator Bowl.

Coach Jordan had decided before the Gator Bowl that the 1975 season, his twenty-fifth as head coach at Auburn, would be his last. Although he had privately shared the decision with Lee Haley, then Auburn's Athletic Director, and President Philpott, he intended to publicly announce his retirement just before the first game of the season. Jordan felt that he had another strong team and he didn't want speculation over his future being a distraction during the season. He also felt that if the announcement was made before the season, instead of after, he could have some control over who would be named his successor. Jordan wanted someone on his staff to be hired to succeed him and many believe he wanted defensive coordinator Paul Davis, who was also the Assistant Head Coach and had previously been the head coach at Mississippi State, to be his successor.

But Coach Jordan's plan for the public announcement of his retirement went awry in April of 1975. In a meeting of the University Board of Trustees that month, he confided to the board members that the 1975 season would be his last and that he intended to announce it publicly just before the season. But while gathered together, the trustees used the meeting to begin considering who would be named as Jordan's replacement. Just a few months removed from the thrashing of Texas in the Gator Bowl, the sentiment of the board quickly centered on Doug Barfield, whose veer offense had just ripped through the mighty Longhorns. Thus, within minutes of privately announcing his retirement, the Board of Trustees decided upon his replacement. Coach Barfield was chosen as Auburn's next head football coach before he even knew for certain the job would be coming open or that he was a leading candidate.

The word of this decision was leaked out to the media by one of board members within hours, forcing Coach Jordan to hold a press conference the following day to make the public announcement of his pending retirement several months earlier than he had intended and on the same day that Doug Barfield was publicly announced as his successor. Looking back, the actions of the Board of Trustees to the news of his retirement – rushing to name a replacement within minutes and then leaking the confidential information to the media within hours – had to be a great disappointment to Coach Jordan and showed little respect for the man, a Word War II veteran of the D-day invasion of Normandy, and all he had accomplished for Auburn over more than two decades.

The decision to hire Doug Barfield Jordan's successor before the start of the season likely caused dissension and mixed loyalties among the coaching staff during the 1975 season. While expectations were high at the start, the team underperformed with a 4 – 6 – 1 season. It was only the third losing season in Coach Jordan's twenty-five years at Auburn. He finished with a career record of 176 – 83 – 6, the third-best record of any SEC coach, and was voted into the college football Hall of Fame.

As the 1976 season lay ahead, Doug Barfield was now the man in charge of Auburn football. But for all his support among members of the Board of Trustees, it seems Coach Barfield wasn't prepared for the being a head coach in the SEC. His resume was fairly thin. He had been offensive coordinator at Clemson for two seasons before taking the job as coach of the freshman team at Auburn, then had been the offensive coordinator for the 1974 and 1975 seasons.

You have to wonder why instead of Barfield, Auburn did not look to former player and Jordan assistant Vince Dooley, the Georgia head coach. Dooley had taken over as head coach at Georgia in 1964, won SEC championships in both 1966 and 1968, and would win another in 1976. Dooley would later turn down the offer Auburn made to him in 1981 when Coach Barfield was fired, but five years earlier could have been the right time for Auburn to bring him home.

Coach Barfield's first Auburn team in 1976 made no improvement over the prior season and finished 4 – 7. The 1977 team showed improvement on offense, but not on defense and the record was only 6 – 5. The 1978 team is not notable for its 6 – 4 – 1 record but for the fact that it lost games while playing William Andrews, Joe Cribbs, and James Brooks at running back (occasionally all at the same time in a triple option attack), all of whom would go on to star in the National Football League.

With both Cribbs and Brooks each rushing for over 1000 yards in 1979, Auburn went 8 – 3, had a final ranking of sixteenth, and it appeared Auburn might be turning the corner. A new upper deck at Jordan-Hare Stadium added 11,000 seats and raised its capacity to almost 73,000. But that hope was short-lived after Tennessee beat Auburn 42 – 0 in the third week of the 1980 season. Auburn finished 5 – 6 overall and 0 – 6 in the SEC, and Coach Barfield was relieved of his duties.

The Auburn football program was once again in need of rebuilding. It had gone more than twenty years without a national championship season, though several opportunities had arisen between 1969 and 1974 that Coach Jordan had just not been able to fulfill. After giving one of Shug's own staff the opportunity in 1976, this time Auburn's leadership searched nationally for its new football coach. Auburn managed to hire the right man, who wasn't from that far away after all.

8

COACH PAT DYE AND THE 1983
NATIONAL CHAMPIONSHIP SEASON

When Auburn looked for a new head coach to replace Doug Barfield, the sights were set first on Georgia's head coach Vince Dooley. Dooley had quarterbacked Shug Jordan's first Auburn team and had served as one of his assistant coaches for several years. His Georgia team had just finished the season undefeated behind the power running of freshman Herschel Walker and was playing for the 1980 national championship. While Dooley was interested in the Auburn job, he was ultimately too settled at Georgia after fifteen years. Dooley ended up using Auburn's great interest in him to leverage Georgia into giving the additional title of Athletics Director.

After losing out on Dooley, Auburn's search committee spoke with several potential candidates, including Jackie Sherill of the University of Pittsburgh and Bobby Bowden of Florida State University. But no one wanted the job as much as Pat Dye, who had just finished a year in the head coaching job at the University of Wyoming after having been head coach at East Carolina University for seven years. To show how much he wanted the job, Dye resigned as Wyoming's head coach even before being offered the position by Auburn.

A former Georgia player and assistant coach to Bryant at Alabama, Dye told the search committee that he knew Auburn's football fortunes were tied to beating Georgia and Alabama, that he had been a part of those programs, and that he knew what it took to beat them. Dye got the job, and he quickly proved that his word was good; he did indeed know how to win. The Auburn football program was rebuilt quickly on the same kind of foundation used by Coaches Donahue and Jordan, a tough and physical team led by a strong defense and a conservative power running offense.

While fans were optimistic, a winning season was not expected for Pat Dye's first Auburn team in 1981. James Brooks, the one star of Barfield's last team, was now a rookie in the NFL and there was no player of his caliber on the 1981 squad. Auburn finished with the same 5 – 6 record in 1981 that it had in 1980, but two of the wins were against SEC opponents, LSU and Florida.

The Auburn team showed vast improvement in Coach Dye's second season, finishing 9 – 3, with a bowl game win over a Boston College team led by Heisman Trophy winner Doug Flutie and a final ranking of fourteenth. The young star of the team was freshman running back Vincent "Bo" Jackson, who possessed a rare combination of size, power, and speed. But the best sign that the Auburn football program had taken an important step forward was a 23 – 22 victory over Alabama, keyed by Jackson's game-winning, fourth-down touchdown dive now referred to since as "Bo over the top." The win ended Auburn's nine-game losing streak to Alabama and established that Dye's teams would be able to compete head to head with Alabama, which had just won a national championship in both 1978 and 1979.

Given the success of the 1982 team and the fact most of its best players were returning, expectations for Pat Dye's third Auburn team were very high. The 1983 squad included five players that would be named both All-SEC and All-American: running back Bo Jackson, offensive tackle Pat Arrington, defensive linemen Donnie Humphrey and Doug Smith, and linebacker Gregg Carr. Five more players would be named to an All-SEC team: Defensive linemen Dowe Aughtman and Gerald Robinson, defensive back David King, offensive lineman David Jordan, and running back Lionel James.

But the excitement for the season had to be tempered by the fact that Auburn faced a schedule that was ranked by the NCAA as the very toughest in the nation. The Billingsley Report, whose computer formula is used in the BCS poll, would later rate Auburn's 1983 schedule as the fifth most difficult in the entire history of college football. Auburn's players would face that schedule in tribute to their fallen teammate Greg Pratt, who had collapsed and died after completing a series of pre-season conditioning runs. Against a gauntlet that included seven teams that would finish in the Top 25 of the A.P. poll, including four Top Ten teams, Auburn would honor Pratt by finishing 11 – 1, winning the Southeastern Conference championship, and being named a national champion by the New York Times computer poll, and many other recognized selectors, including the Fleming System, James Howell's Rankings, the Billingsley Report, the Massey Ratings of Kenneth Massey, 1st-N-Goal, the Dolphin Historical College Football Rankings, the Hatch Mathematical College Football Rankings, the Nutshell Sports

Football Ratings, and the Sparks Achievement Ratings. The NCAA's Official Records book also recognizes the Auburn Tigers as a national champion for 1983.

Auburn opened the 1983 season on September 10 at home in Jordan-Hare Stadium before over 73,000 fans against a strong University of Southern Mississippi team that would finish the season with an 8 – 3 record. Auburn scored quickly when Lionel James made an eight yard touchdown run after Greg Carr had recovered a Southern Miss fumble. While the Golden Eagles responded with a field goal, Bo Jackson added a 10 yard touchdown run and a 44 yard touchdown reception from quarterback Randy Campbell. Despite Bo Jackson's two touchdowns, the star of the game was the diminutive James, who ran for 172 yards on just 16 carries.

On September 17, Auburn hosted a University of Texas team that was then ranked third in the country and which would go on to finish 11 – 1, win the Southwest Conference championship, and have a final ranking of fifth after a bowl game loss to Georgia. Auburn wasn't quite ready at the start of the game and Texas jumped out to a 20 – 0 first half lead and ended up winning 20 – 7. While the loss was disheartening, given the difficulty of Auburn's schedule it would have plenty of opportunities to demonstrate how good a team it could be.

Up next for Auburn was a September 24 game against Tennessee in Knoxville. Since the 1950's Auburn and Tennessee had played early in the season and the game was a good gauge of the strengths of the teams and the kind of season they would have. Auburn rebounded from the loss to Texas with a strong showing on the road, despite the fact that Tennessee had not played the previous week and had two weeks to prepare for the Tigers. Tennessee had a veteran team and great hope for the season and for this game the team was clothed in special all-orange uniforms to give the Volunteer players an additional spark. Auburn jumped out to a 7 – 0 lead with a short run by Bo Jackson for a touchdown, then grew the lead to 10 – 0 with a field goal by kicker Al Del Greco. Tennessee responded with a 30 yard touchdown pass to receiver Tim McGee and the score was 10 – 7 at halftime. In the second half Auburn added a two-yard touchdown run by Randy Campbell and another Del Greco field goal to bring the score to 19 – 7. The game was broken open for Auburn when Trey Gainous returned a punt 81 yards for a touchdown. While Tennessee would add a touchdown, Auburn responded with a touchdown run on a reverse by Clayton Beauford and Del Greco's third field goal of the day to bring the final score to 37 – 14. By defeating by such a wide margin a Tennessee team that would go on to finish the season at 9 – 3 and a final ranking of twenty-first, Auburn proved it was much better than it had showed against Texas.

On October 1, Auburn, which had risen to number ten in the polls, faced Florida State University in Jordan-Hare Stadium. Bobby Bowden was building a powerful football program in Tallahassee and his Seminoles team, then ranked seventeenth, was a strong test for the Tigers. Like Tennessee, FSU had an off week the week before playing Auburn and thus had two weeks to prepare for the game. Auburn scored first on a Randy Campbell pass to tight end Jeff Parks, but Florida State responded with a short touchdown pass and a field goal to take a 10 – 7 lead. Al Del Greco's field goal kicking proved crucial for Auburn all season, and he added two second quarter field goals. After fullback Tommie Agee took a Randy Campbell pass in for a 27 yard touchdown, Auburn had a 20 – 10 lead at halftime.

In the second half, Florida State's Kelley Lowrey ended two long drives with quarterback sneaks for touchdowns and the Seminoles carried a 24 – 20 lead into the last minutes of the game. However, Auburn was able to move the ball on a long drive, converting on two fourth down plays. With just under two minutes to play, Campbell hit Lionel James with a short pass that he was able to run in for a 15 yard touchdown. The 27 – 24 Auburn victory was preserved when Greg Carr intercepted a pass with the Seminoles within field goal range. Though he did not score a touchdown, Bo Jackson was Auburn's offensive star, rushing for 123 yards on just 15 carries. Florida State would go on to finish the season with an 8 – 4 record and a final ranking of twenty-fifth.

Auburn traveled to Lexington for their next game on October 8 against the University of Kentucky before the largest crowd in Commonwealth Stadium history. The Kentucky game was the third game in a row that Auburn's opponent had an off week the week before and thus two weeks to prepare for Auburn. The extra preparation didn't do the Wildcats much good, as the Tigers more than doubled their score and won 49 – 21. Auburn scored six rushing touchdowns, three by Bo Jackson, two by quarterback Randy Campbell, and one by his backup, Mike Mann. Even Auburn's defense scored, as David King intercepted a pass and retuned it 40 yards for a touchdown. Despite the lopsided score, Kentucky fielded a winning team in 1983, went to a bowl game, and finished 6 - 5 -1.

Auburn next faced its old rival Georgia Tech, with the October 15 game played at historic Grant Field in Atlanta, site of match-ups between the teams dating back to Coaches Donahue and Heisman. Auburn entered the game having moved to fifth in the polls, but played uninspired and trailed 10 – 7 at halftime. Auburn's touchdown had come on a 13 yard run by Tommie Agee. Auburn looked ripe for an upset when a fumble on the first play of the second half led to a field goal that extended Georgia Tech's lead to 13 – 7. However, Coach Dye gave the team a halftime tongue-lashing that inspired them to play their best and that was all the scoring Tech would do. With Bo Jackson rushing for 123 yards on 18 carries, Auburn stormed back for a runaway 31 – 13 victory.

On October 22, fifth-ranked Auburn faced Mississippi State at home. The Tigers did not get off to slow start this time, jumping ahead by the score of 14 – 0 on two first quarter touchdowns. Lionel James scored on a 74 yard run, and then Bo Jackson scored on a short pass from Randy Campbell. Mississippi State added a pair of field goals before Auburn put the game away with touchdown runs by Tommie Agee and Brent Fullwood. With a 28 – 13 victory, Auburn's raised its record to 6 – 1, but its next three games would be against teams ranked in the top ten in the nation.

After the victory against Mississippi State, Auburn moved up a spot to the fourth spot in the national rankings. Next on the schedule was an October 29 game against the fifth-ranked Florida Gators before a sell-out crowd at Jordan-Hare Stadium. The game is memorable in the lore of college football for the fact that fifty-one of the players on the field that day would be signed to NFL teams, including eleven players who would be first-round draft choices and twenty-two who would become NFL starters. The player who shined brightest among the college football stars that day was sophomore running back Bo Jackson, who rushed for rushed for 196 yards on only 16 carries.

Auburn jumped out to a 14 – 0 lead on a 55 yard touchdown run by Jackson and then a short running touchdown by Randy Campbell. Florida responded with a long touchdown pass from Wayne Peace to Ricky Nattiel. Auburn's next scoring drive was led by Lionel James, as he accounted for 54 of the 80 yards, including a 17 yard run for the touchdown. Trailing 21 – 7, Florida looked to get back in the game when Randy Campbell threw an interception. It looked like Gator running back Neal Anderson had scored on a short run, but the referee recognized that Auburn safety Tommy Powell had stripped the ball from Anderson just before he crossed the goal line. Auburn was rewarded with a touchback and the ball was placed on the twenty yard line. Before the Florida fans could settle down, either from still celebrating a score or from criticizing the referee's call taking the score away, Bo Jackson broke loose, outran the Gator defense with word-class speed and scored on an 80 yard run. Thus, what could have been a 21 – 14 game, was suddenly 28 - 7. While Florida added two touchdowns in the fourth quarter, it was not enough and Auburn defeated a Florida team that would finish 9 - 2 – 1 and end up ranked sixth in the country.

The great difficulty of Auburn's football schedule in 1983 is best symbolized by the fact that its Homecoming opponent on November 5 was not some "creampuff" team providing a guaranteed win for returning alumni, but the seventh ranked University of Maryland Terrapins led by "Boomer" Esiason, who would go on to star as an NFL quarterback. Third-ranked Auburn jumped out to a 14 – 0 lead on a pass by Campbell to Chris Woods and a 61 yard run by fullback Tommy Agee. But Maryland rallied to take a 17 – 14 lead on two touchdown passes by Esiason and a short field goal. Auburn responded with a short touchdown run by Bo Jackson and another long touchdown run by Agee to take a 28 – 17 lead. Tommy Agee would finish the game with 219 yards on 24 carries. Esiason brought Maryland back, completing an 80 yard scoring drive late in the game that left the score at 28 – 23 when a two-point play attempt failed. Auburn added to its lead near the very end of the game when Esiason was hit and fumbled in his own end zone and the ball was recovered by defensive lineman Donnie Humphrey for a touchdown and the 35 – 23 final score. Maryland would go on to finish the season with an 8 – 4 record.

Auburn's next game on November 12 was in Athens against the three-time defending SEC champion Georgia Bulldogs. The game between third-ranked Auburn and fourth-ranked Georgia was the biggest game between the schools in more than a decade, as the winner would clinch the SEC championship. The game in Sanford Stadium before a sellout crowd and a national television audience was a defensive slugfest. Auburn scored first on a short touchdown run by Lionel James, then added two Del Greco field goals to build a 13 – 0 lead. That score held until late in the fourth quarter Georgia when avoided a shutout by completing a touchdown on a pass from John Lastinger to Herman Archie for the 13 – 7 final score. Once again, Bo Jackson was key for the offense, as he rushed for 118 yards on 18 carries. Auburn's margin of victory should have been even greater, but the usually reliable kicker Al Del Greco missed three field goal attempts.

After clinching at least a tie for the SEC championship with the win over Georgia, Auburn did not play again until its December 3 game at Legion Field in Birmingham against the nineteenth-ranked University of Alabama. A win over Alabama would complete a 6 – 0 SEC schedule and assure an outright SEC Championship, instead of sharing it with both Georgia and Alabama. In a nationally-televised game, Bo Jackson rose to the occasion and led Auburn to a 23 – 20 victory with two long touchdown runs and a total of 256 yards gained rushing on only 20 carries. With much of the game played in a rainstorm that would lead to a tornado warning at the stadium, Jackson's second touchdown run of 71 yards was aptly described by Alabama coach Ray Perkins as a "strike of lightning" to his team. Auburn's defense also played well that day, as safety Victor Beasley intercepted the Tide's star quarterback Walter Lewis twice, and kicker Al Del Greco regained his usual form by converting three field goal attempts that ultimately decided the game.

Auburn played in the January 2, 1984 Sugar Bowl against the eighth-ranked University of Michigan Wolverines who were led by legendary coach Bo Schembechler. A win in the game would give third-ranked Auburn, who had played the nation's toughest schedule, a great chance to win the national championship. But Michigan was a particularly difficult match-up for Auburn, as the Wolverines boasted a top-ranked rushing defense and the Auburn offense was designed around being able to run the football out of a wishbone option attack.

Michigan also had a high scoring offense and quickly took a 7 – 0 lead when a long first quarter drive ended with a short touchdown run by quarterback Steve Smith. While the Auburn defense shut down the Michigan offense the rest of the game, their job was made more difficult by four turnovers committed by the Tiger offense that killed potential scoring drives. Auburn's offensive game plan was to match its strength against Michigan's strength and rely on its running game. Despite a Michigan defense stacked to stop the run, Coach Dye was so determined to run the ball that quarterback Randy Campbell only attempted six passes the entire game. While Auburn did ultimately prove successful by gaining over three-hundred yards rushing, the offense did not score a touchdown. Despite having a strong statistical advantage, Auburn could only muster two short Al Del Greco field goals and trailed 7 – 6 when the offense took possession of the football on its own thirty-nine yard line with under eight minutes left in the game.

Despite the pressure caused by trailing on the scoreboard, Auburn didn't change its run-only game plan and alternated between halfbacks Bo Jackson and Lionel James, and fullback Tommie Agee, who rushed for thirty-four yards on the drive. When Bo Jackson was stopped just short of the Michigan goal line as time was running out, Coach Dye sent in Del Greco for the chip-shot, game-winning kick and a 9 – 7 Sugar Bowl victory. Once again, Auburn was paced by the rushing of Bo Jackson, who finished with 130 yards on 22 carries against Michigan's run-stacked defense.

The day seemingly worked out perfect for Auburn, ranked third nationally, to win a national championship. Both teams ranked ahead of it in the polls lost their bowl games and no teams remained undefeated. Just prior to the Sugar Bowl, Georgia, who Auburn had defeated just weeks earlier, beat number two ranked Texas in the Cotton Bowl. Later that evening, fifth-ranked University of Miami beat the number one ranked University of Nebraska in the Orange Bowl by one point and the path to number one had been cleared for Auburn. However, the next morning, the Associated Press and the United Press International surprisingly jumped Miami over Auburn and named it national champion.

However, the New York Times, which had a history of making a final ranking of college teams going back into the 1920's, and used a sophisticated computer program that factored in strength of schedule, named Auburn as the national champion. So did many other recognized selectors, including the Fleming System, James Howell's Rankings, the Billingsley Report, the Massey Ratings of Kenneth Massey, 1st-N-Goal, the Dolphin Historical College Football Rankings, the Hatch Mathematical College Football Rankings, the Nutshell Sports Football Ratings, and the Sparks Achievement Ratings.

The 1983 Auburn team is well-deserving of the title of national champion, more so than Miami, the only other recognized champion. While both Auburn and Miami finished 11 – 1, Auburn had faced a more difficult schedule and thus the quality of its wins were superior. Miami had only played six teams with winning records, while Auburn played nine such teams, a vast difference. While Miami had played only five of the teams in the final A.P. Top 25 ranking, Auburn played seven such opponents. While Miami played only two teams in the final A.P. Top 10, Auburn played four Top 10 teams, three of those in its last five games.

Miami and Auburn played three common opponents in 1983, Florida, Florida State, and Mississippi State. Auburn defeated the Gators 28 – 21, while Miami lost, 28 – 3. Miami's twenty-five point blowout loss was the largest margin of defeat ever suffered by a team that went on to be named national champion. By comparison, Auburn's only loss in 1983 was a 20 – 7 defeat to then third-ranked Texas, half as large a margin of defeat. By any head-to-head comparison, Auburn had a season that was not just equivalent to Miami's, but actually one that was far superior.

Miami was awarded the national championship in the aftermath of its exciting, narrow victory over then number one ranked Nebraska in the Orange Bowl, its own home field. While Nebraska had been considered the preeminent team that season, review of its record shows that Nebraska had gone undefeated and into the number one spot by feasting on mediocre teams until it played Miami. While Nebraska played eight teams with winning records in 1983, it played only one team other than Miami that finished ranked in the final A.P. Top 20 ranking. Thus, Nebraska's status was based upon playing a soft schedule, it was not truly as strong a team as was it was then considered to be. Thus, Miami's narrow victory over the Cornhuskers – as exciting as it may have been at the time – is not as meaningful as it was then believed by the voters and is insufficient as support award Miami a national championship instead of Auburn.

Given a proper perspective, Auburn should *not* have been jumped by Miami in the polls and Auburn should have been voted number one by the A.P. and U.P.I. It no accident that the rankings of selectors such as the New York Times, James Howell, and the Billingsley Report, that utilized mathematical formulas utilizing a strength of schedule factor rather than human emotions in the aftermath of a single game, recognized Auburn as the 1983 national champion.

Richard Billingsley, whose computer formula has been used in the BCS rankings and who is an NCAA_recognized national championship selector, has called for Auburn to claim a national championship for 1983.

In sum, Auburn is a national champion for 1983 because it was the SEC Champion; played by far the most difficult schedule in the nation that year that is now recognized as the fifth most difficult schedule in college football history; was led by superstar athlete Bo Jackson; and was chosen as national champion by at least ten recognized selectors, and is recognized as a national champion for 1983 by the NCAA. The 1983 national championship should be claimed by Auburn's Athletic Department with a banner in Jordan-Hare Stadium.

9

THE REMAINING COACH DYE ERA:
SEC DOMINANCE

After the 1983 national championship season, Auburn would field strong teams for all but the last two years of Coach Pat Dye's tenure at Auburn. Expectations for the 1984 team were soaring and Auburn was chosen number one in the preseason polls. Auburn added a strong recruiting class of freshman to a team that returned stars like running back Bo Jackson. But Bo Jackson suffered a shoulder injury in the second game against the University of Texas, and the final record of 9 – 4, highlighted by a wild 42 - 41 victory over Florida State in Tallahassee, failed to meet expectations. The 1985 season was similar and was highlighted by a 59 – 27 win over Florida State and a 24 - 10 win over Georgia. Though expectations remained high and Bo Jackson had an amazing season that would lead to him being named the Heisman Trophy winner, the team finished only 8 – 4, signaling a need for some changes in the program.

When Coach Dye took over the program in 1981, he instituted a wishbone, triple option running offense that he had first learned as an assistant coach to Bear Bryant. By 1984, Dye had switched the offense to more of an I-formation attack where Bo Jackson could be used at tailback and be a threat to run on either side of the field. The result was that in 1985, Jackson was able to fully demonstrate his many outstanding talents by rushing for 1786 yards on just

286 carries and winning the Heisman Trophy. But in hindsight there hadn't been enough wins given the sheer number of talented players on those teams.

Like Coach Jordan before him, Coach Dye had to realize that he was going to have to adapt his approach to the game and throw the football more to have greater success. So Dye hired Auburn's Heisman Trophy-winning quarterback, Pat Sullivan, to be the quarterback coach and share offensive coordinator duties with Larry Blakeny. Dye also elevated linebacker coach Wayne Hall to be defensive coordinator. Those coaching changes reinvigorated the program and led to Auburn dominating SEC football in the last half of the 1980's.

In 1986, running back Brent Fullwood, who had played in Bo Jackson's shadow, had his chance to star and rushed for 1391 yards on just 167 carries for just over an eight yard per carry average. Fullwood finished fourth in the Heisman Trophy voting. Jordan-Hare Stadium was expanded again in 1987, with a second upper deck raising capacity to 85,000 seats. With an expanding passing attack from new quarterback Jeff Burger to receivers such as Lawyer Tilllman, Auburn had a outstanding 10 – 2 season marred only by narrow losses to Florida and Georgia. Although the 4 – 2 SEC record was only good for a second place finish, Auburn finished sixth in the final A.P. poll, and the coaching changes had been a success.

With Burger returning at quarterback and a strong defense in 1987, Auburn went 9 – 1 – 2, won the SEC championship, and finished seventh in the final A.P. poll. Led by defensive tackle Tracy Rocker, winner of both the Outland and Lombard trophy awards, Auburn's defense was dominant in 1988. With Reggie Slack at quarterback,

Auburn continued to have a balanced offense without a true star running back, and Auburn finished the 1988 season at 10 – 2, repeated as SEC champion, and was ranked eighth in the final A.P. poll. However, that season will be forever remembered for the frustration of losing the "Earthquake game" against LSU in Baton Rouge by the score of 7 – 6 on a last minute touchdown pass. That loss kept Auburn out of a bowl game matchup against Notre Dame for the national championship, a game Auburn would have likely won given its dominant defense and Notre Dame's one-dimensional running offense.

Auburn's run of great success continued in 1989, even though there were only a few returning starters. Auburn finished 10 – 2 for the second year in a row, won a third straight SEC championship, and finished sixth in the final A.P. poll. However, 1989 will always be remembered as the first year that Alabama, then ranked number two, traveled to Auburn to play in Jordan-Hare Stadium. Auburn won the game 30 – 20 before a record crowd, and celebrated a day that Alabama officials had sworn would never happen.

With the end of the 1980's also came an end to the dominance of the Auburn football program in the SEC. With freshman Stan White at quarterback in 1990, Auburn finished 8 – 3 – 1, and managed a Top 20 ranking in the final A.P. poll. But the program stumbled to a 5 – 6 record in 1991 as a former player alleged he had received improper benefits while at Auburn. The NCAA began an investigation and Auburn managed a similar 5 – 5 – 1 record in 1992. Like Coach Jordan, Pat Dye fought a serious illness late in his coaching career, and he resigned at the end of the 1992 season.

In retrospect, Coach Dye's career at Auburn was amazingly similar to that of Coach Donahue, which had ended exactly seventy years earlier. While Donahue won four conference championships over eighteen years and finished with a 99 – 35 – 5 career record, Dye won four conference championships over twelve years, with an almost identical career record of 99 – 39 – 4.

10

COACH TERRY BOWDEN AND THE
1993 NATIONAL CHAMPIONSHIP SEASON

With Pat Dye's resignation at the end of the 1992 season, Auburn was forced to search for a new head football coach while waiting on the NCAA's response to alleged rules violations. Two of the frontrunners for the position were Dick Sheridan, who had just lead North Carolina State University to successive nine win seasons, and Fisher DeBerry, who two years earlier had led the Air Force Academy to a 10-win season that included a bowl game victory over Mississippi State. But Sheridan ended up retiring from his position at North Carolina State due to health issues and 1992 was his last year as a football coach. DeBerry decided to stay at Air Force, where he continued as head coach for another fourteen years.

The surprise pick of the Auburn search committee was Terry Bowden, the head coach at Division I-AA Samford University and the son of Florida State coach, Bobby Bowden. Bowden had coached his Samford team to a 21 – 5 record the prior two seasons and at the young age of thirty-seven, already had nine years experience as a head coach. Bowden brought excitement and optimism to a program that the NCAA had just put on two year's probation, including a bowl ban.

In 1992, the Southeastern Conference added the University of Arkansas and the University of South Carolina and split the teams into two, six team divisions. Auburn was placed in the Western Division, along with Alabama, Arkansas, LSU, Mississippi State, and Ole Miss, while the Eastern Division was composed of Florida, Georgia, Kentucky, South Carolina, Tennessee, and Vanderbilt. With this conference structure and a new eight game conference schedule, Auburn retained annual games with Alabama and Georgia, but lost its traditional games with Tennessee and Florida. Auburn also gained annual games with LSU and Ole Miss, teams it had not often played in recent decades. Under this new structure, each division would have a champion, which would then play in a conference championship game. In 1992, Alabama had defeated Florida on the way to winning a national championship.

While the expectations for the 1993 Auburn team were not great, the team actually had many great players who were not recognized as such when the season started. But they would be by year's end. Quarterback Stan White, a senior and a four-year starter, was the most experienced quarterback in the conference. The many young players that had started for Auburn in the prior two losing seasons, before they were truly ready for SEC competition, now had game experience to add to their talent. Offensive tackle Wayne Gandy and punter Terry Daniel would both be named to All-American and All-SEC teams, and offensive tackle Anthony Redmon, running back James Bostic, kicker Scott Etheridge, and defensive backs Chris Shelling and Calvin Jackson would be named to All-SEC teams. Bowden hoped to eventually open up Auburn's offensive philosophy to be more like his father's at Florida State, but also retained Wayne Hall as defensive coordinator to maintain consistency on the defense.

With a young and enthusiastic head coach, the 1993 Auburn team refused to accept low expectations and along the way learned how to win, even facing a schedule the NCAA had rated in the preseason as one of the toughest in college football. Auburn finished the season 11 – 0, and was named national champion by several recognized selectors, including the National Championship Foundation, Nutshell Sports Football Ratings, David Wilson's Retro-Ratings, and the Sparks Achievement Ratings. The NCAA Official Records book recognizes this Tiger squad as a national champion for 1993.

The season opened with a Thursday night game in Auburn on September 2 against the University of Mississippi, who had beaten Auburn the prior season. Auburn got on the scoreboard first with a short field goal by Scott Etheridge. Then defensive tackle Mike Pelton recovered an Ole Miss fumble, which set up a short touchdown run by James Bostic. Another Etheridge field goal gave Auburn a 13 – 0 lead at halftime. Auburn added a field goal in the third quarter to take a 16 – 0 lead into the fourth quarter. Ole Miss got back in the game when it capitalized on an Auburn fumble by quickly throwing a long touchdown pass. After Ole Miss failed on a two-point conversion attempt, the score was 16 – 6. Auburn ran the football and the clock to try and hold onto a win, but the conservative strategy almost didn't work. With just three minutes left in the game, Ta'Boris Fisher of Ole Miss returned a Terry Daniel punt 77 yards for a touchdown to bring the score to 16 – 12, after another two-point conversion failed. Auburn held on for the 16 – 12 win over an Ole Miss team that would finish the season with a winning record (6 – 5). Auburn was led in the game by the efforts of running back James Bostic, who rushed for 138 yards on 28 carries and would become the workhorse for the team and a star in the SEC.

On September 11, Coach Terry Bowden and his new team faced his old one, the Samford Bulldogs. Auburn won easily, and Bowden held down the final score to 35 – 7. Frank Sanders caught two touchdown passes, Thomas Bailey added a touchdown reception, and freshman running back Stephen Davis, a future NFL-All Pro player, had two touchdown runs and 122 yards on 18 carries.

Auburn's next game on September 18 was against LSU in Baton Rouge. LSU jumped out to an early 7 – 0 lead, but Coach Bowden opened up the passing game and Stan White led the team to a 21 – 7 lead at halftime. White scored on a quarterback sneak and then later threw a long touchdown pass to Thomas Bailey. James Bostic accounted for the other touchdown with a 13 yard run. White added another quarterback sneak for a touchdown in the third quarter, and Scott Etheridge kicked a field goal for a 31 – 7 lead. LSU could only add a field goal, that was matched by Etheridge in the fourth quarter to give Auburn a 34 – 10 victory. The Auburn offense had exploded with over 500 yards of offense, with White completing 20 of 28 passes for 281 yards. James Bostic ran for 110 yards on just 13 carries and Davis added ninety-five more yards on the ground. Auburn showed that it had the players for a potent offense that could move the ball by both the running and passing game, a nightmare for defenses.

Auburn next played the University of Southern Mississippi on September 25 before a crowd of 84,000 in Auburn. The Auburn team might have been looking back on the LSU game rather than thinking about the task at hand with Southern Miss because the offense had six turnovers on the day, including a fumble on the first play from scrimmage that led to a 7 – 0 lead for the Golden Eagles. But Auburn responded with three touchdowns to take a 21 – 7 lead at halftime. James Bostic scored twice on short runs and Stephen Davis added the third score. The third quarter all but belonged to Southern Miss, as they added a touchdown pass, a field goal, and the returned an interception of a Stan White pass for a touchdown to take a 24 – 21 lead. But Auburn regained the lead with a 38 yard touchdown pass from White to Thomas Bailey and then added a fourth quarter touchdown from Bostic to seal a 35 – 24 victory.

Auburn traveled to Nashville on October 2 to take on Vanderbilt. Although Vanderbilt's teams always played hard, they generally did not fare well against SEC competition in the 1990's. This game was almost a different story for the Commodores, as Auburn played poorly and the defense had to make a four play, goal line stand late in the fourth quarter to preserve a narrow 14 – 10 comeback victory. Auburn's touchdowns came on an interception return by safety Brian Robinson and a two yard run by James Bostic.

Auburn returned home for an October 9 game against Mississippi State. The Bulldogs took a 6-0 lead at the end of the first quarter based on two field goals. But Auburn responded with three touchdown passes from Stan White in the second quarter to take a 21 – 6 halftime lead. White hit Frank Sanders with a 57 yard pass, then Stephen Davis scored a screen play, and Tony Richardson, a future NFL All-Pro player, caught a short pass for a touchdown. When Mississippi State added a field goal, Auburn responded with a short touchdown by Richardson to bring the lead to 28 – 9. The Bulldogs added a touchdown and two-point conversion in the fourth quarter, but Scott Etheridge added a field goal for Auburn and the final score was 31 – 17. With six wins, Auburn had already exceeded its win total from each of the prior two years and Auburn football was exciting again.

However, a huge test lay ahead in Jordan-Hare Stadium on October 16 in the form of the visiting fourth ranked Florida Gators led on the field by star quarterback Danny Weurffel and coached by former Heisman Trophy winner Steve Spurrier. But in the first six games Auburn had demonstrated a strong running game led by the bruising runner James Bostic and emerging star Stephen Davis, as well as a big play passing game with Stan White and receivers Thomas Bailey and Frank Sanders. It would be up to the defense to try and slow down Florida's SEC-leading offense to give Auburn a chance to win.

Florida looked to break the game open in the first quarter as the Gators got a long field goal on their first possession, then added a 60 yard touchdown pass from Weurffel to Willie Jackson to take a 10 – 0 lead. The Gators defense had stymied Auburn's running game and the offense looked to extend that lead when still in the first quarter they drove to Auburn's ten yard line. But defensive back Calvin Jackson cut in front of a Weurffel pass intended for Willie Jackson in the end zone, intercepted the ball, and ran untouched for a 96 yard touchdown to cut Florida's lead to just 10 – 7. Auburn then took a 14 – 10 lead as Stan White scored on a quarterback sneak after a long drive where

Coach Bowden had begun to rely more Stan White's passing than the power running game. But Florida responded with seventeen straight points on a field goal, a run by Errict Rhett and a Weurffel touchdown pass to build a 27 – 14 lead at halftime. Auburn edged closer with a third quarter score on a pass from Stan White to fullback Tony Richardson to bring the score to 27 – 21. Auburn took a 28 – 27 lead early in the fourth quarter when after a long drive, James Bostic broke a tackle in the backfield on a fourth down play from the Florida one yard line and powered in for a touchdown. It looked like Florida was going to retake the lead, but Auburn defensive back Chris Shelling intercepted a Weurffel pass and returned it 65 yards to the Florida nine yard line. From there, receiver Frank Sanders scored on a reverse and Auburn's lead was extended to 35 – 27, But Florida came back on the passing of Danny Weurffel and scored a touchdown and two-point conversion to tie the game with five minutes left. White then led Auburn on a 50 yard drive that set Scott Etheridge up for a 41 yard, game-winning field goal that brought the final score of Auburn 38, Florida 35. Florida would beat Alabama in the SEC Championship game and finish the season 11 – 2. After the upset victory and with a 7 – 0 record on the season, Auburn moved into the A.P. Top 10.

After a week off, Auburn traveled to Fayetteville for an October 30 game against the University of Arkansas under icy, frigid conditions. Auburn started the game with a nice drive, but Scott Etheridge's field goal attempt into the wind was short. Arkansas then took its first possession in for a touchdown to take a 7 – 0 lead. After a 56 yard Stan White to Frank Sanders pass completion, White made a one-yard plunge for a touchdown to tie the score at the half. Auburn took the lead early in the third quarter when an Arkansas receiver slipped on the icy turf and Brian Robinson intercepted and ran 35 yards for a touchdown. Auburn extended the lead to 17 – 7 on an Etheridge field goal, but Arkansas added a long touchdown pass to narrow the score. However, Auburn pulled away in the fourth quarter with touchdown runs by Bostic and fullback Reid McMilion, who would, reminiscent of a Mike Donahue fullback, rush up the middle for a career high 91 yards on 12 carries. Though Arkansas added a late touchdown, the Auburn team earned a hard-fought 31 – 21 victory over an Arkansas team that would finish 6 - 4 -1.

Up next for Auburn on November 6 was its Homecoming game with New Mexico State. This was an easy 55 – 14 victory for the Tigers. Auburn was led by quarterback Stan White, who threw three touchdown passes, and James Bostic who rushed for 104 yards on only 11 carries. With the win, Auburn, then 9 – 0 on the season, moved to number seven in the A.P. poll.

Auburn traveled to Athens on November 13 for a game with its oldest rival, the Georgia Bulldogs, who were a slight favorite at home. Georgia was led by star quarterback Eric Zeier and a strong group of receivers such as Hanson Graham. Auburn scored on its first possession, taking a 7 – 0 lead on a 28 yard run by fullback Tony Richardson. Georgia responded with a long drive that ended with a one-yard touchdown run by future NFL All-Pro Terrell Davis. In the second quarter, Auburn added two touchdown runs by James Bostic to take a 21 – 7 lead into halftime. In the third quarter, Auburn extended the lead when Chris Shelling intercepted a tipped pass and ran it 73 yards for a touchdown. Georgia responded with a 76 yard touchdown pass from Zeier to Hanson Graham to bring the score to 28 –

14. But then Auburn drove the ball 80 yards for a score, with Stan White passing to Frank Sanders for a touchdown. In the fourth quarter, Georgia would come within seven points when Zeier threw for another touchdown, but Bostic would add a final touchdown run to make the final score 42 – 28. Bostic would finish the game with 183 yards rushing on just 19 carries.

On November 20, the University of Alabama team, defending national champions, traveled to play in Auburn for just the second time. Auburn scored first on a short field goal by Scott Etheridge late in the first quarter. But Alabama took the lead when Kevin Lee ran for 62 yards for a touchdown on a reverse. However, Auburn's defense was able to sack Alabama quarterback Jay Barker for a safety to bring the score to 7 – 5. Alabama extended its lead to 14 – 5 when running back Chris Anderson scored on a 19 yard run just before halftime.

Auburn's defense would regroup at halftime and returned to the field to dominate Alabama in the second half. Auburn would draw closer even after star quarterback Stan White was injured and had to leave the game midway through the third quarter. Facing a fourth and long from Alabama's 35 yard line, Coach Bowden sent in backup quarterback Pat Nix with instructions to throw a long pass play. Nix floated the ball deep to Frank Sanders, who out-jumped his defender, pulled the ball in on the three yard line, then dove into the endzone. Suddenly, Auburn only trailed by the score of 14 – 12, and momentum had swung to the Tigers.

The Tigers took the lead for good early in the fourth quarter when Etheridge added a short field goal. Then, late in the game, as Auburn was simply trying to run out the clock and hold the narrow 15 – 14 lead, James Bostic exploded through a hole on a run up the middle and, weaving between Alabama defenders, ran 70 yards for a touchdown that brought the final score to 22 – 14.

Thus, a season that started with a "no name" team that hoped to have a winning season had star players emerge that would dominate in the SEC and Auburn finished with a perfect 11 – 0 record. Because Coach Bowden accomplished the undefeated season with an experienced roster of players brought into the program by Coach Dye, many people don't give Coach Bowden enough credit for his role as leader of that team simply because years later he would leave Auburn with his reputation tarnished. But his willingness to expand the passing offense and his abilities as a "game day" coach were critical to Auburn's success. As Coach Dye stated after the Alabama game, he couldn't have coached the team to an undefeated season, and history shows that he was right. Coach Dye never had an undefeated team. So when we think of the 1993 season, much credit has to be given to Coach Bowden for infusing the program with new optimism and for his ability to lead the team to victory in every game, often having to come from behind.

Though Auburn was ineligible for the SEC championship game or a bowl game because of a sanction of NCAA probation, it had defeated both Florida, who was the winner of the Eastern Division, and Alabama, who was named the winner of the Western Division, to finish as the only undefeated team in the SEC. Auburn was voted fourth in the final A.P. poll, but was named national champion by at least three recognized selectors, including the National Championship Foundation, Nutshell Sports Football

Ratings, and David Wilson's College Football Performance Ratings. Moreover, the NCAA also recognizes Auburn as a national champion for 1993.

The most widely accepted national champion for the 1993 college football season appears to be Florida State University. The Seminoles finished the season 12 – 1, with a loss to the University of Notre Dame, but beat previously unbeaten Nebraska in a bowl game. Notre Dame had finished 11 – 1 and was recognized as the national champion by a few selectors. While both FSU and Notre Dame had outstanding seasons, both lost games during the regular season, while Auburn played a strong schedule, remained undefeated, and beat both participants in the SEC Championship game. While it is true that due to NCAA sanctions Auburn was unable to play in a bowl game, probation and a bowl game sanction does not disqualify a team from being recognized as a national champion. For example, in 1974 the University of Oklahoma was on probation and received a bowl ban, yet was named national champion by the A.P. poll.

In sum, Auburn is a national champion for 1993 because, with an 11 – 0 record, the team was unbeaten against a tough SEC schedule that featured two Top Ten teams and was named national champion by several selectors and is recognized as a national champion by the NCAA as well. The undefeated 1993 Auburn team is deserving of the title of a national champion and that championship should be claimed by Auburn's Athletic Department with a banner in Jordan-Hare Stadium.

11

THE REMAINING COACH BOWDEN ERA:
THE INEVITABLE FALL

Terry Bowden's tenure as the head football coach at Auburn University began with such great promise in 1993, but ended in disappointment just five years later when, after a 1 – 5 start, he resigned mid-season because he believed he would not be retained as head coach when the season ended. With the benefit of two decades of hindsight it's easy to see that such success achieved so rapidly was unlikely to be lasting. But, at the time one had to wonder where, after an incredible 11 – 0 initial season, things went wrong.

The 1994 season began with high expectations and 1993's eleven game winning streak continued for the first nine games of 1994, a period when it seemed Auburn would find a way to win every game. But the streak ended with a 23 – 23 tie against Georgia when Auburn's kicker missed a game-winning field goal. The season ended with a 21 – 14 loss to Alabama, which left Auburn with a 9 -1 -1 record in 1994.

Coach Bowden had stated when he had been named head coach at Auburn that he wanted an offense like his father's at Florida State and a defense like Pat Dye had had at Auburn. By his third year at Auburn, Bowden had begun transitioning the offense away from a balanced attack that featured a power running game with future NFL running backs like James Bostic, Stephen Davis, Tony Richardson, and Fred Beasley to a pass-first offense and a finesse style running game with smaller and quicker backs. That offense was simply not as consistent in the SEC and the losses began to mount when Bowden also failed to maintain a strong defensive unit.

Auburn was predicted to contend for that national championship in 1995, but the team did not live up to those expectations. The result was an 8 - 4 record in both 1995 and 1996 that made fans sense the program had slipped substantially since the players Bowden had inherited, the foundation of the 1993 and 1994 teams, were no longer on the team.

A closer examination of Auburn's SEC record indicates that this was true, as an 8 – 0 record in 1993 had steadily fallen to 6 - 1 – 1 in 1994, 5 – 3 in 1995, and 4 - 4 in 1996. During that time, Bowden had transitioned Auburn's offense from a power running style favored by Coach Dye to a pass-first, finesse style that he preferred, but which history has showed is difficult to win with against the SEC's powerful defenses. In the SEC, even a passing-based offense must be balanced by a strong running game.

Auburn's football fortunes improved in 1997 behind the amazing quarterback play of senior Dameyune Craig, who was tailor-made for Bowden's offense and who seemed to almost single-handedly lead the team to a 6 – 2 SEC record, a Western Division championship, and a matchup in the SEC championship game against Tennessee. But Tennessee, behind the play of its own star quarterback

Peyton Manning, edged by Auburn by a score of 30 – 29, and after a bowl win, Auburn finished the season at 10 – 3.

Auburn fans expected that the 1998 season would be a bit of a rebuilding year because Dameyune Craig and other key players from the 1997 team had been seniors. But no one expected the team open the season being shut out at home by a mediocre University of Virginia team, and to struggle to a 3 – 8 season and a 1 – 7 SEC record with a cupboard of players that seemed bare of stars. And no one expected that after the team's 1 - 5 start, Coach Bowden would resign and the team would have to be turned over to defensive coordinator Bill Oliver as interim head coach to finish out the season. Once again, the Auburn football program was at a crossroads.

12

COACH TOMMY TUBERVILLE AND THE 2004 NATIONAL CHAMPIONSHIP SEASON

Bill "Brother" Oliver, a former Alabama player, assistant coach, and defensive coordinator, finished the final five games of the 1998 season with a 2 – 3 record as Auburn's interim head coach. It was an usual situation because Oliver, who had also been a defensive backfield coach at Auburn for Coach Jordan in the late Sixties, wanted the job permanently and lobbied heavily for it. But Auburn's search committee had their sights set on another candidate to replace Terry Bowden. That coach was Tommy Tuberville, who had just guided the University of Mississippi through several years of NCAA probation with severe sanctions and who had been named the SEC Coach of the Year in 1997. When he accepted the responsibility of being Auburn's new head coach, Tuberville was faced with having to rebuild the football program from the ground up.

Even though Auburn had won the Western Division Championship in 1997, Tuberville discovered his 1999 squad was severely lacking in talented players. Despite that, his first Auburn team showed some improvement, going 5 – 6, with wins over LSU and Georgia that suggested better days lay ahead. Then with the addition of junior college transfer

Rudi Johnson, a bruising running back who played much like former star James Bostic and who would later star in the NFL, Auburn won the SEC Western Division in 2000 and finished the season with a 9 – 4 record.

Auburn fans expected even more in 2001, but Johnson had opted to enter the National Football League draft, and Auburn's record fell to 7 – 5. In the aftermath of a 31 – 7 upset loss to Alabama at home that some fans still call "Black Saturday," Tuberville replaced both his offensive and defensive coordinators. With the new coordinators, Bobby Petrino and Gene Chizik, Auburn improved to 9 – 4 in 2002 and expectations were exceptionally high for the 2003 season. Coach Tuberville had brought talented players into the program for several years and preseason predictions had Auburn ranked as high as number one. With stars on offense and defense, Auburn fans were expecting another berth in the SEC championship game. But Petrino left Auburn after the 2002 season to take a head coaching job, and Tuberville gave the offensive coordinator position to two of his assistants to share. That decision ultimately proved a disastrous one, as Auburn was unproductive on offense all season, despite having many talented players. As a result, the 2003 the team stumbled to a disappointing 8 – 5 record. Only an exciting win over archrival Alabama, the third in four years under Coach Tuberville, ended up saving him his job.

In the wake of the disappointing season where the offense was unproductive, Coach Tuberville hired an experienced offensive coordinator, Al Borges. Borges brought a "West Coast" style of offense to Auburn that emphasized running the football along with a precise short yardage passing game that occasionally went deep.

Tuberville and the 2004 team prepared to meet the expectations that the 2003 team had failed to fulfill. Because many of the star players from the 2003 season were returning for the 2004 season, expectations were still high.

The 2004 squad included four players that would be named to both All-SEC and All-American teams: running back Carnell Williams, offensive tackle Marcus McNeil, and defensive backs Carlos Rogers (who would win the Jim Thorpe Award as the nation's best defensive back) and Junior Rosegreen. More players would also be named to the 2004 All-SEC team, including quarterback Jason Campbell, running back Ronnie Brown, center Danny Lindsey, and linebacker Travis Williams. Following the season, Brown, Williams, Campbell and Rodgers would all be drafted in the first round of the NFL draft.

But the excitement for the season had to be tempered based on the fact that the schedule included LSU, the defending national champion, as well as old rivals Tennessee, Georgia, and Alabama. However, despite that difficult schedule, what unfolded was a magical undefeated season in which Auburn finished 13 – 0 and was named national champion by at least two recognized selectors.

Auburn, ranked seventeenth in the A.P. preseason poll, opened the season on September 4 with a game at home against the University of Louisiana-Monroe before 83,000 fans. While ULM was not expected to provide much competition, Auburn's offense had been unproductive the prior year and it was taken as a good sign when the Auburn offense was able to score four touchdowns while still learning the new offense. Carnell Williams rushed for 103 yards on 23 carries, Jason Campbell threw two touchdown passes, and Auburn won 31 – 0.

Auburn traveled to Starkville for its next game on September 11 against Mississippi State, who was led by the SEC's first African-American head coach, Sylvester Croom, who had starred as a player at Alabama. The Bulldogs has opened their season with a win against Tulane and their fans believed they could win at home against Auburn. But Auburn quickly took control of the game with two first quarter touchdowns, as Anthony Mix caught a short pass from Jason Campbell and Carnell Williams scored on a one yard run. Campbell threw a 25 yard touchdown pass to Ben Obomanu in the second quarter and Auburn led 21 – 0 at halftime. Auburn added three touchdowns in the second half to build a 43 – 0 lead. Campbell threw a long touchdown pass to Mix, Williams scored on another short run, and backup quarterback Brandon Cox got in the game long enough to throw a touchdown to Obomanu. Mississippi State added two touchdowns in the fourth quarter against Auburn's reserve defense, to bring the final score to 43 – 14. Both of Auburn's great running backs had big days as Ronnie Brown rushed for 147 yards on just 15 carries and Williams ran for 122 yards on 19 carries.

On September 18, Auburn hosted LSU in Jordan-Hare before a crowd of that exceeded normal stadium capacity. The fifth-ranked LSU Tigers were defending national champions, were on a ten game winning streak, and had defeated Auburn the year before in Baton Rouge by a 31 – 7 score. LSU got on the scoreboard first with a short touchdown pass from quarterback Marcus Randle to Dwayne Bowe, but the extra point kick was missed and Auburn only trailed 6 – 0. Auburn responded with a short field goal by kicker John Vaughn to cut LSU's lead to 6 – 3. Early in the second quarter, LSU added a long field goal to build a 9 – 3 lead. From there, the game that had been dominated by the defenses turned into a pure defensive struggle.

When LSU had to punt the ball and Auburn took over on its own 41 yard line with a little over six minutes remaining in the game, Auburn fans knew this could be their team's last chance to score the touchdown needed to win. Auburn moved the ball to LSU's twenty-six yard line with a 20 yard run Brown, a scramble by Campbell and a pass to Williams. But the LSU defense then bowed up and Auburn faced a fourth down and twelve that could decide the game. Under heavy pressure from blitzing LSU defenders, Campbell stood poised and at the last instant threw a bullet to Courtney Taylor. Taylor made a clutch catch and Auburn had a first down at the LSU fourteen yard line. On third down, Campbell found Taylor open in the back of the end zone for a touchdown. After an LSU penalty negated a miss of the extra point attempt, Auburn was give another opportunity. John Vaughn then kicked the crucial extra point and came away with a narrow 10 – 9 victory over an LSU team that would finish 9 – 3 on the season and have a final ranking of sixteenth in the A.P. Poll. It would be closest Auburn would come to losing a game all season.

Auburn's next game was at home against the Citadel, a Division I-AA school that would not be much competition. Auburn scored quickly, led 23 – 0 at halftime, then played reserves and won by a 33 – 3 score. Auburn had been scheduled to play Bowling Green University, but it got out of the contract in order to play the University of Oklahoma for a larger payout. The Citadel is the only team Auburn could schedule as a replacement on short notice.

On October 2, Auburn traveled to Knoxville to play the undefeated and tenth-ranked Tennessee Volunteers before a crowd of 108,000 in Neyland Stadium and a national television audience. Auburn jumped out to a quick 7 – 0 lead when Ronnie Brown scored on 9 yard run. Tennessee responded with a long field goal, but Auburn took a 14 – 3 lead when Jason Campbell throw a short touchdown pass to Ben Obomanu just before the end of the first quarter. The lead jumped to 31 - 3 at halftime as Auburn added a John Vaughn field goal, a touchdown run by Carnell Williams, and a touchdown pass from Campbell to Courtney Taylor. Tennessee scored a touchdown in the fourth quarter and Auburn added a field goal to bring the final score to 34 – 10. While Campbell had had a big game passing for Auburn, his counterparts for Tennessee, Erik Ainge and Brent Schaefer, combined to throw five interceptions to the Auburn defense, with four of those by safety Junior Rosegreen. Auburn had now been tested and two Top Ten teams and passed each test and moved to sixth in the rankings.

Auburn's next game, at home against Louisiana Tech University, was on October 9. Although Tech was not a strong opponent, Auburn did what a good team is supposed to do when playing inferior competition and scored quickly, taking a 24 – 0 lead at halftime. Even Auburn's defense had taken part in the scoring as star defensive back Carlos Rodgers intercepted a pass and returned it for a touchdown. Auburn played reserves for most of the second half and won by a score of 52 – 7.

On October 16, number four ranked Auburn hosted the University of Arkansas before a crowd of 87,000 in Jordan-Hare Stadium. As it had been doing most of the season, Auburn's offense dominated right from the start of the game and built a 17 - 0 lead in the first quarter and then led 30 – 7 at halftime. The first quarter was highlighted by long touchdown passes from Jason Campbell to Devin Aromashodu and Courtney Taylor, and a field goal by John Vaughn. Auburn then turned to its running game as both Ronnie Brown and Carnell Williams each added a touchdown before Arkansas's quarterback Matt Jones threw a touchdown pass. In the second half, Jason Campbell threw a touchdown pass to Ben Obomanu and Arkansas added two more scores as Auburn won comfortably 38 - 20. Jason Campbell had a stellar game passing as he completed 17 of 19 passes, including three touchdowns. Ronnie Brown added 101 yards rushing on just 15 carries and Auburn had over 500 yards of offense for the second time that season.

Auburn's next opponent, on October 23, was at home the University of Kentucky. The game followed the seemingly regular script of the all the games so far that season, except for LSU: Auburn would open up the offense and take a sizeable lead into halftime, add to the lead in the third quarter and then run conservative plays to run out the clock and preserve the win. Auburn fans were beginning to refer to the conservative change in offensive play calling in the second half as the offense going into the "Tubershell." Against Kentucky, number three ranked Auburn took a 21 – 0 lead in the first quarter based on two touchdown runs by Carnell Williams and one by Ronnie Brown. Kentucky scored a touchdown in the second quarter and the score was 21 - 7 at halftime. Kentucky kicked a field goal early in the third quarter to draw a bit closer, but then Brown and backup fullback Carl Stewart added touchdown runs for Auburn to bring the score to 35 – 10. In the fourth quarter, the Auburn defense added a score of its own as backup linebacker Kevis Burnam a recovered a Kentucky fumble and scored to bring the finally tally to 42- 10. Carnell

Williams had led the way for the Tigers with 149 yards on just 17 carries.

On Auburn 30, Auburn traveled to Oxford to take on the University of Mississippi. The Auburn offense was inconsistent in the first half and only took a 7 – 0 lead at halftime when Jason Campbell scored on a quarterback sneak after leading the team on a 99 yard drive. Auburn moved ahead 14 – 0 on a short touchdown run by Ronnie Brown and after that Auburn and Mississippi alternated touchdowns before Auburn built a 35 – 14 lead that would be the final score. While Jason Campbell did not have a great game passing, Brown and Carnell Williams were strong running the football and each ran for about 100 yards and scored a touchdown.

Auburn faced the fifth-ranked University of Georgia Bulldogs before a crowd of 87,000 fans in Jordan-hare Stadium and a national television audience on November 13. While the game was expected to be a battle between two equally strong teams, Auburn once again dominated from the start. On its first possession Auburn drove the ball 80 yards for a 7 – 0 lead, with Carnell Williams scoring from one yard out. Georgia blocked a punt and threatened to score and tie the game, but an interception by Carlos Rodgers ended that drive. Auburn scored in the second quarter on a halfback pass from Williams to Anthony Mix for a touchdown and also added a field goal to make the score 17 – 0 at halftime. In the fourth quarter, Auburn added a touchdown pass from Jason Campbell to Ronnie Brown to bring the score to 24 – 0. Georgia added a late touchdown pass, but the two point conversion attempt failed. Auburn had a 24 – 6 win over a Georgia team that would finish the season 10 – 2 and ranked seventh. Campell played spectacular in the game, completing 18 of 22 passes, and Williams added 101 yards on 19 carries.

On November 20, Auburn traveled to Tuscaloosa for a game against in-state rival Alabama before a crowd of 83,000 in Bryant-Denny Stadium. This game played out almost the opposite of earlier games, as Coach Tuberville kept the offense in the Tubershell in the first half even though the Alabama defense was stacked to stop the running plays he was having called. As a result Auburn fell behind on the scoreboard. Alabama moved the ball well but was eventually thwarted by Auburn's defense and had to settle for two field goals and a 6 – 0 lead at halftime.

However, Auburn wasted little time taking the lead in the second half as Coach Tuberville opened up the offense to let Coach Borges run it as he had done in the first half in previous games. Jason Campbell was called on to attempt deep passes against the Alabama defense crowding the line of scrimmage. That strategy worked to perfection as Auburn quickly scored touchdowns on its first three possessions of the second half. On the first possession, Campbell hit Devon Aromashodu with a 51 yard pass and had an 80 yard drive capped by a short Carnell Williams touchdown run for a 7 – 6 lead. Campbell then hit Courtney Taylor with a 32 yard pass for a 14 – 6 lead. On the third possession, Campbell hit Taylor on another long pass and Ronnie Brown scored on a short run for a 21 – 6 lead. Alabama added a late touchdown pass to bring the final score to 21 – 13. Auburn had finished its regular season SEC schedule at 8 – 0, was undefeated, and as winner of the Western Division would face Eastern Division winner Tennessee for the second time in the SEC Championship game.

The SEC Championship game was played on December 4 in the Georgia Dome in Atlanta. The game started much like the prior game between the two teams as Auburn jumped out to an early lead. Auburn moved the ball 86 yards for a touchdown score in just four plays on its first possession, then went 66 yards on nine plays to take a 14 – 0 lead midway through the first quarter. But Tennessee took advantage of a mistake by Auburn's punter, recovered the ball on Auburn's fourteen yard line, and scored on a two yard run by Cedric Houston. Auburn responded with another long drive that ended with Jason Campbell throwing to Courtney Taylor for a short touchdown that made the score 21 – 7.

In the second half, Tennessee scored again off of an Auburn miscue. Early in the third quarter, Campbell fumbled and a few plays later the Volunteers added a touchdown pass to make the score 21 – 14. On Tennessee's next possession, Gerald Riggs found an opening and ran 80 yards for a touchdown to tie the game at 21 – 21. But Auburn responded with a long drive capped by a 53 yard touchdown pass from Campbell to Devin Aromashodu. Auburn then added a short field goal that extended the lead to 31 – 21. Tennessee was able to add another touchdown run by Riggs, but Auburn responded with another touchdown pass by Campbell, this time to Ben Obomanu. The touchdown brought the final score to 38 – 28, and Auburn had its fourth win over teams that would end the season ranked in the Top Twenty. Campbell was the star of the game for Auburn, completing 27 of 35 passes for nearly 400 yards and adding 57 yards rushing.

Although Auburn was undefeated (12 - 0) and the SEC Champion, because it had started with a preseason ranking of seventeen – while the University of Southern California and the University of Oklahoma had started the season ranked first and second and had also remained undefeated -- Auburn was edged out of a spot in the BCS Championship game. This occurred because the voters in the human polls would not elevate Auburn above the other two teams as long as they remained undefeated, and at least one computer formula used in determining the BCS rankings used preseason rankings as a part of its formula, which penalized Auburn for something it could not control. Auburn, as SEC Champion was paired in the Sugar Bowl with Virginia Tech, the Atlantic Coast Conference champion, which had finished the regular season with a 10 – 2 record and was ranked ninth.

The 2005 Sugar Bowl was played in New Orleans on January 3 before a sellout crowd of over 77,000 fans and a nationwide television audience. This would be a game featuring two great defenses. While Auburn was ranked first nationally in allowing the fewest points per game, Virginia Tech was third ranked, and while Auburn was fifth ranked in allowing the fewest yards gained per game, Virginia Tech was ranked fourth. Both defenses were at their best in this game.

After stopping Virginia Tech on its first drive, the Auburn offense started fast again as Jason Campbell hit tight end Cooper Wallace with a 35 yard pass and then Ronnie Brown ran for 31 yards. Auburn got the ball inside the Hokies' ten yard line, but could only get a John Vaughn field goal to take a 3 – 0 lead. On Tech's second drive, quarterback Marcus Randle threw a pass that was intercepted by Auburn safety Junior Rosegreen, who returned the ball 31 yards. Campbell completed a 23 yard pass to Courtney Taylor, but the drive stalled inside the Tech ten yard line once again. Vaughn kicked another short field goal and Auburn led 6 – 0 at the end of the first quarter. The defenses controlled for much of the second quarter, but then Randle completed a series of passes that gave Tech first-and-goal at the Auburn two yard line. The Auburn defense stopped three running plays and then on fourth down Tech's coach, Frank Beamer, declined a field goal attempt. Instead, he had Randle try a pass on fourth down that fell incomplete and Auburn's defense had held. Auburn took the ball over on its one yard line and, behind Campbell's passing, again drove inside Tech's ten yard line. But the offense couldn't score and Vaughn kicked a third field goal to take a 9 – 0 lead at halftime.

Auburn started its first possession of the second half with runs by Carnell Williams and Ronnie Brown, then Campbell hit Anthony Mix with a 53 yard pass. Auburn scored a few plays later on a pass from Campbell to Devin Aromashodu to take a 16 – 0 lead. Late in the quarter, a Campbell pass was intercepted and the Hokies began a drive that would end with a missed field goal. The fourth quarter began with Auburn leading 16 – 0. However, Tech began to move the ball as Randle passed on almost every play and he completed a 29 yard touchdown pass to Josh Morgan. The two point conversion attempt failed and Auburn's lead was cut to 16 – 6 with seven minutes remaining in the game. Tech got the ball back on its twenty yard line with two minutes left and scored on an 80 yard pass to Morgan to bring the final score to 16 – 13.

Auburn finished a 13 – 0 season in which had it had defeated four teams ranked in the Top Ten when they played and five teams that would finish in the Top Twenty (counting both games played against Tennessee).

In the BCS Championship game, Southern California defeated Oklahoma by the score of 55 - 19 and was voted national champion in the A.P. Poll, as well as by other selectors. Auburn, with its 13-0 record and Southeastern Conference championship, finished second in the BCS standings, the A.P. Poll, and the Coaches Poll (formerly the U.P.I. Poll), but was named as national champion by several newer selectors, including Darryl Perry and the GBE College Football Ratings. Auburn is certainly deserving of a national championship claim based on these facts, but especially because of what occurred subsequently.

In 2010, Southern California was stripped of the 2004 BCS Championship title when the NCAA placed the program on probation for rules violations that occurred during that season and included improper benefits being provided to one of its star players, Reggie Bush. The receipt of the improper benefits made Bush ineligible as a student athlete during that season and, as a result, the NCAA penalty for the rules violations included vacating all of Southern California's wins and the loss of the BCS championship. The Football Writers Association of America, which awards a national championship trophy, also stripped the Trojans of that championship. However, the A.P. took no action in regards to Southern California's 2004 A.P. national championship.

Although Auburn had a legitimate right to claim a National Championship for 2004 even before Southern California's BCS championship and FWAA championship were vacated by those organizations, once that occurred Auburn's right to claim a national championship for the

2004 season became even stronger. There should be a national champion recognized for the 2004 college football season, and Auburn is plainly the most deserving team.

Auburn has the right to claim a national championship because it played a stronger schedule than either Southern California or Oklahoma, won all of its games and usually dominated. While Southern California played four games against teams rated in the final A.P. Top Twenty and Oklahoma only played three such games, Auburn played five games against teams in the final Top Twenty. Auburn played seven teams that finished with winning records and played in bowl games, the same as Southern California, while Oklahoma played just six such teams.

In sum, Auburn is a national champion for 2004 because, with a 13 – 0 record, it was unbeaten against a schedule that featured two Top Ten-rated teams and five total Top Twenty teams, a more difficult schedule than that played by either Southern California or Oklahoma, and was named national champion by not just one, but several recognized selectors. The undefeated 2004 Auburn team is deserving of the title of a national champion based on those facts alone, but is especially deserving because Southern California's BCS championship was vacated. The Auburn Athletic Department should claim a national championship for the 2004 season with a banner in Jordan-Hare Stadium.

13

IN CLOSING

I hope that this book provides Auburn University students and alumni, as well as other fans of Auburn's football program, with a better understanding and appreciation for its great football history. In addition to the 1957 and 2010 teams, there are seven additional Auburn football teams – those in 1910, 1913, 1914, 1958, 1983, 1993, and 2004 – that are worthy and deserving of being called a national champion. I am not alone in this view. In addition to 1957 and 2010, the NCAA also recognizes Auburn as a national champion for 1913, 1983, and 1993, and all the teams discussed in this book have been named a national champion by recognized selectors while also meeting the standard of being either conference champion, undefeated, or both. Perhaps Auburn fans and alumni will advocate for recognition of those teams by Auburn's Athletic Department so that Auburn will change its current stance and claim all nine national championships, or at least all five recognized by the NCAA Other universities have recently claimed additional national championships for past seasons. Auburn should not hesitate to do the same.

However, even if readers are not convinced that any of the seven teams written about in this book are worthy of being called a national champion, the discussion and debate of the subject of what is a college football national champion and which teams are deserving of claiming that title in any year should be entertaining to anyone who enjoys college football history. This book is intended to add to such a discussion and should be considered with that spirit in mind.

APPENDIX:
AUBURN'S NATIONAL CHAMPION SEASONS

1910

6 - 1 Record (5 - 0 in SIAA) Southern Intercollegiate Athletic Association Co-Champion

10/8   AU 6   MISS STATE 0 @ Auburn
10/15 AU 77   HOWARD (now Samford) 0   @ B'ham
10/22 AU 17   CLEMSON 0   @ Auburn
10/29 AU 0   TEXAS 9   @ Austin, TX
11/5   AU 16   GA TECH 0   @ Atlanta, GA
11/12 AU 33 TULANE 0   @ New Orleans, LA
11/24 AU 26   GEORGIA 0 @ Savannah, GA

1913

8 - 0 Record (8 - 0 in SIAA) Southern Intercollegiate Athletic Association Champion

10/4   AU 53   MERCER 0 @ Auburn
10/11 AU 55   FLORIDA 0   @ Auburn
10/18 AU 20   CLEMSON 0 @ Clemson, SC
10/25 AU 34   MISS STATE 0 @ B'ham
11/1   AU 7   LSU 0 @ Mobile
11/8   AU 20   GA TECH 0   @ Atlanta, GA
11/15 AU 14   VANDY 6 @ B'ham
11/22 AU 21   GEORGIA 7 @ Atlanta, GA

1914

8-0-1 Record (5 - 0 - 1 in SIAA)

9/26   AU 39   MARION 0 @ Auburn
10/3   AU 60   HAMILTON 0 @ Auburn
10/10   AU 20   FLORIDA 0 @ Jacksonville, FL
10/17   AU 28   CLEMSON 0 @ Auburn
10/24   AU 19   MISS STATE 0 @ Auburn
11/7   AU 14   GA TECH 0 @ Atlanta, GA
11/14   AU 6   VANDY 0 @ B'ham
11/21   AU 0   GEORGIA 0 @ Atlanta, GA
12/5   AU 7   CARLISLE 0 @ Atlanta, GA

1957

10 – 0 Record (7 – 0 in SEC) Southeastern Conference Champion, A.P. National Champion

9/28   AU 7   TENNESSEE 0 @ Knoxville, TN
10/5   AU 40   CHATTANOOGA 7 @ Auburn
10/12   AU 6   KENTUCKY 0 @ Auburn
10/19   AU 3   GEORGIA TECH 0 @ Atlanta, GA
10/26   AU 48   HOUSTON 7 @ Houston, TX
11/2   AU 13   FLORIDA 0 @ Auburn
11/9   AU 15   MISS STATE 7 @ B'ham
11/16   AU 6   GEORGIA 0 @ Columbus, GA
11/23   AU 29   FLORIDA ST 7 @ Tallahassee, FL
11/30   AU 40   ALABAMA 0 @ B'ham

1958

9 – 0 – 1 Record (6 – 0 – 1 in SEC)

9/27	AU 13	TENNESSEE 0 @ B'ham
10/4	AU 30	CHATTANOOGA 8 @ Auburn
10/11	AU 8	KENTUCKY 0 @ Lexington, KY
10/18	AU 7	GEORGIA TECH 7 @ Atlanta, GA
10/25	AU 20	MARYLAND 7 @ Auburn
11/1	AU 6	FLORIDA 5 @ Gainesville, FL
11/8	AU 33	MISS ST 14 @ Auburn
11/15	AU 21	GEORGIA 6 @ Columbus, GA
11/22	AU 21	WAKE FOREST 7 @ Auburn
11/29	AU 14	ALABAMA 8 @ B'ham

1983

11 – 1 Record (6 – 0 in SEC) Southeastern Conference Champion

9/10	AU 24	SO. MISS 3 @ Auburn
9/17	AU 7	TEXAS 20 @ Auburn
9/24	AU 37	TENNESSEE 14 @ Knoxville, TN
10/1	AU 27	FLORIDA ST 24 @ Auburn
10/8	AU 49	KENTUCKY 21 @ Lexington, KY
10/15	AU 31	GEORGIA TECH 13 @ Atlanta, GA
10/22	AU 28	MISS ST 13 @ Auburn
10/29	AU 28	FLORIDA 21 @ Auburn
11/5	AU 35	MARYLAND 23 @ Auburn
11/12	AU 13	GEORGIA 7 @ Athens, GA
12/3	AU 23	ALABAMA 20 @ B'ham
1/2	AU 9	MICHIGAN 7 @ New Orleans, LA

1993

11 – 0 Record (8 – 0 in SEC)

9/2	AU 16	OLE MISS 12	@ Auburn
9/11	AU 35	SAMFORD 7	@ Auburn
9/18	AU 34	LOUISIANA STATE 10	@ Baton Rouge, LA
9/25	AU 35	SO. MISS 24	@ Auburn
10/2	AU 14	VANDERBILT 10	@ Nashville, TN
10/9	AU 31	MISS STATE 17	@ Auburn
10/16	AU 38	FLORIDA 35	@ Auburn
10/30	AU 31	ARKANSAS 21	@ Little Rock, AR
11/6	AU 55	NEW MEXICO ST 14	@ Auburn
11/13	AU 42	GEORGIA 28	@ Athens, GA
11/20	AU 22	ALABAMA 14	@ Auburn

2004

13 – 0 Record (9 – 0 in SEC) Southeastern Conference Champion

9/4   AU 31   LA. MONROE 0 @ Auburn
9/11   AU 43   MISS STATE 14 @ Starkville, MS
9/18   AU 10   LOUISIANA STATE 9 @ Auburn
9/25   AU 33   CITADEL 3 @ Auburn
10/2   AU 34   TENNESEE 10 @ Knoxville, TN
10/9   AU 52   LA TECH 7 @ Auburn
10/16 AU 38   ARKANSAS 20 @ Auburn
10/23 AU 42   KENTUCKY 10 @ Auburn
10/30 AU 35   OLE MISS 14 @ Oxford, MS
11/13 AU 24   GEORGIA 6 @ Auburn
11/20 AU 21   ALABAMA 13 @ Tuscaloosa, AL
12/4   AU 38   TENNESSEE 28 @ Atlanta, GA
1/3   AU 16   VIRGINIA TECH 13 @ New Orleans, LA

2010

14 – 0 Record (9 – 0 in SEC) Southeastern Conference Champions, BCS Champion

9/4	AU 52	ARK. STATE 26	@ Auburn
9/9	AU 17	MISS. STATE 14	@ Starkville, MS
9/18	AU 27	CLEMSON 24	@ Auburn
9/25	AU 35	SOUTH CAROLINA 27	@ Auburn
10/2	AU 52	LA. MONROE 3	@ Auburn
10/9	AU 37	KENTUCKY 34	@ Lexington
10/16	AU 65	ARKANSAS 43	@ Auburn
10/23	AU 24	LOUISIANA STATE 17	@ Auburn
10/30	AU 51	OLE MISS 31	@ Oxford, MS
11/6	AU 62	CHATTANOOGA 24	@ Auburn
11/13	AU 49	GEORGIA 31	@ Auburn
11/26	AU 28	ALABAMA 27	@ Tuscaloosa, AL
12/4	AU 56	SOUTH CAROLINA 17	@ Atlanta
1/10	AU 22	OREGON 19	@ Phoenix, AZ

ABOUT THE AUTHOR

Michael Skotnicki earned two degrees from Auburn University in the 1980's, and taught at Auburn as an Instructor for one year. He also graduated *magna cum laude* from the Cumberland School of Law of Samford University, served as a law clerk and then staff attorney to several justices of the Alabama Supreme Court for several years, and has practiced law in Birmingham, Alabama for more than fifteen years.